# HOW
# TO
# GET
# TOP
# DOLLAR
# FOR
# YOUR
# HOME
# IN GOOD
# TIMES
# OR BAD

Also by Irving Price

*Buying Country Property*

# HOW TO GET TOP DOLLAR FOR YOUR HOME IN GOOD TIMES OR BAD

## *Irving Price*

Times
BOOKS

Published by TIMES BOOKS, a division
of Quadrangle/The New York Times Book Co., Inc.
Three Park Avenue, New York, N.Y. 10016

Published simultaneously in Canada by
Fitzhenry & Whiteside, Ltd., Toronto

**Library of Congress Cataloging in Publication Data**

Price, Irving.
   How to get top dollar for your home.

   1. House selling.  I. Title.
HD1379.P737    333.33'8    79-91654
ISBN 0-8129-0901-1

Manufactured in the United States of America

To my family
and all of the nice people
who made this book possible

# Contents

HOW
TO
GET
TOP
DOLLAR
FOR
YOUR
HOME
IN GOOD
TIMES
OR BAD

# I
# *What to Do Until the Broker Comes*

# 1

## *What Your Broker May Not Tell You*

Homes are sold every day. In fact, as you read this very page, negotiations for thousands of home sales are under way across the country...some for Top Dollar, but, unfortunately, many more for less.

Sure, I realize that the market isn't so great today. Why, I can't open a newspaper or a magazine without seeing more gloom and doom about the mortgage situation—the lack of mortgage money and high interest rates. I hear John Doe tell the evening TV news reporter that he's had his home on the market for three months now, but nary a soul has crossed his threshold. And I listen to some of my fellow brokers, who tell me there's just no way to sell a home today.

But I say, not so. After more than thirty years experience putting buyers and sellers together, as a broker, banker, and real estate consultant, I *know* that no matter what the national or international picture is, in good times or bad, you still can sell your home—and, more than likely, get Top Dollar for it.

No, I cannot agree with the notion that the Great American Dream of home ownership has become a nightmare. If you wake up to reality, that nightmare will quickly vanish.

What is the Big Picture? Well, I'll tell you. Never before have we had more people in the market than the millions today who, for one reason or another—marriage, divorce, retirement, or change of job—need to buy a home and who, more important, are able to support one. No, we're not in a Great Depression; that recession the "experts" have been predicting is questionable. The truth is that employment has never been higher, nor personal income greater. Many families have two, sometimes three incomes. But the situation we do have, as everyone knows, is a shortage of mortgage funds. Even when mortgage money is available, it may be necessary to pay substantial down payments and correspondingly high interest rates. Indeed, you might say that the cost of putting a roof over your head today has gone through the roof.

Naturally, I'm troubled about all of this, and frustrated for both the buyer *and* the seller. On the other hand, I refuse to give up, to close my office, or even to lay off sales people. After all, I can recall having had tough times before, when money was tight or when few people had enough income to buy a home. But we put the sales together then, and we're continuing to do so now.

Believe me, though, this is no pie-in-the-sky or Pollyana-ish philosophy. Actually, it's much easier to play dead and write a book about a coming real estate crash. But I don't believe it, and neither does the prestigious Real Estate Research Corporation of Chicago, which recently reported that the national market is "strong, viable and as healthy as it has been in recent memory."

However, I do know that, if you want to sell a home today, let alone get Top Dollar for it, it's not going to be as easy as it was in years gone by. In those days, all you did was list it with the broker across the street, wait a few weeks, entertain a few offers, and watch your prospective buyer's mortgage application sail through the local money-lending institution. Then you sat back and waited for the closing.

Those days are gone, along with 60-cent-a-gallon gasoline. Just as we've adjusted to rising fuel prices, so must we adjust to the realities of selling a home in the 1980s. For one thing, no longer can we view the problem as belonging to the buyer alone. Today, it is everyone's problem. And yet, if we do a little homework, if we use our imagination and perhaps even make some sacrifices, then we are going to sell those homes.

I am not saying that we have to sacrifice our Top Dollar asking price. It is irrational to dump your home on the market or cut the price tag in half. That won't make your home sell any faster. What you must do is remove the roadblocks that may be keeping your sale from going through—and then go for your Top Dollar. After all, your home deserves it, for, in most areas of the country, the market value of homes has doubled or tripled during the last twenty years. With the cost of new construction at about $60 a square foot, most potential homeowners are trying not to build a nest but to move right into an existing one—such as yours.

This volume is not intended to be an all-encompassing or get-rich-quick text; it's not even a do-it-yourself kit. Hopefully it *is* a clear, concise, down-to-earth, straightforward account of how to sell a home today. Of course, I don't have all the answers, but I have worked eighteen hours a day for more than thirty years in real estate and banking, forever learning as I go along. And life has been pretty good to me. I've made a good living. But, more important, I've had the pleasure of meeting all kinds of interesting people and the challenge of putting together literally thousands of home sales, from the $20,000 raised-ranch to the million-dollar country estate. That is why I feel I can tell you what it takes to sell a home today and, in the process, give you an edge over the competition.

I believe strongly in the Great American Dream of home ownership and the personal security that only a home can bring.

No one can convince me that the home is not the very foundation of this country. So I agree with Ralph Pritchard, President of the National Association of Realtors, when he says that brokers are doing both buyers and sellers a disservice if they advise their clients to wait for home prices or interest rates to come down. It's obvious they will not. In the meantime, homes must be sold. And they will be. That's my credo.

# 2
## *What Is Top Dollar?*

"How did the owners arrive at their asking price?"

We brokers are asked this question nearly every time we show a home to a potential buyer. Furthermore, it is probably the most unanswered question in the real estate business.

Why? Because, in far too many cases, that asking price is not reasonable. Nor has it been based on any concrete, measurable criteria, such as the location of the home, its acreage or plot size, the amount of privacy, or the view, much less the size or physical condition of the house itself. Instead the seller has merely determined a price on some admittedly less tangible basis, perhaps on nothing more than a personal feeling or whim concerning its worth. This they've done without bothering to consult a single appraiser, mortgage banker, or other real estate specialist, and thus their Top Dollar price tag is usually 20 to 30 percent higher than it should be.

Of course, this is not to say that you shouldn't strive for the absolute Top Dollar price for your home. All I'm saying is don't do like so many and overprice it. Remember a *fair* Top Dollar price is the most money your home will bring in competition with others of equal value on the market today. True, I admit it is extremely difficult to find—let alone evaluate—two homes of so-called equal value, but that's all the more reason why you should rely on the professionals for their help in establishing Top Dollar for your home.

In general these professional appraisers follow sophisticated guidelines of evaluation and do the best job possible in a most difficult and non-scientific task. They do not pull figures out of the air arbitrarily but arrive at their opinions by using established, accepted principles of appraisal. One, the "comparable method," also known as the "market data approach," is used by most professionals. It places considerable weight on recent sales of comparable property.

But don't just take one expert's opinion either. You should arrive at a Top Dollar asking price for your home only after seeking numerous opinions from professionals both qualified and knowledgeable in real estate, banking, home building, and market trends. This brain-picking process is sure to be a real learning experience. Once you've evaluated all of the information collected and added a reasonable amount to allow for error, you will come up with an asking price. Only time, circumstance, and luck will tell you if that price is correct—or if you should go back to the drawing board.

However, you will find, if you follow the procedures outlined below, that you will obtain a good cross section of valuable opinion or data on which to base your asking price. And you will do so with a minimum amount of time and cost:

- Seek the opinion of current market value from those in local banking institutions who may or may not be familiar with your specific home.
- Ask the real estate professionals who may be extended a formal listing of your home to give you a good indication of their estimates of a high and low asking price.
- Request an up-to-date review from the insurance agent who

provides coverage for your home. This will give you an indication of current market value, as well as replacement cost. Be guided by the current market value, though, rather than replacement cost, which is often substantially more than the highest asking price.

- Submit an application for the maximum mortgage obtainable from at least one of the leading mortgage-lending institutions in your area. I'll explain later why this, which may cost about $100, is advisable.

- Ask at least three attorneys active in real estate practice to determine the marketability and asking price for your home, and expect to pay a nominal fee. Obviously, it would be helpful if these lawyers were familiar with your home or at least with properties in the area where your home is located.

- Check closely all current listings of homes presently on the market within a reasonable distance. Do not limit your interest only to those homes that are comparable to yours, but review those within all price ranges for general market information. If necessary, discuss a substantial number of these listings with the various brokers offering them in order to obtain additional information.

- Discuss your home and property with at least three locally prominent residential contractors or builders. Try to obtain some indication from them as to present value and replacement cost of your home.

- Visit the managers of your local title insurance companies. They are a good source of information regarding real estate values and activities and are usually most cooperative.

- Discuss your interest in selling your home with one or more real estate investors who buy and sell residential properties as their business. Find out what the home would be worth from an investment standpoint.

- Obtain cost estimates for appraising your home from at least three professional appraisers specializing in residential property. Contact your local Board of Realtors, bank, or attorney for a list of those they would recommend as well qualified members of professional appraising societies. In an effort to keep the cost at a minimum, request a non-detailed appraisal. If the proposal fee submitted is reasonable to you, obtain the appraisal.

- It might also be helpful to visit the officer in charge of the county clerk's office or a similar deed-recording facility in your area. All final real estate transactions are of concern to that office, and thus these individuals are a virtual clearinghouse of information.

As I say, the collection of all this information will indeed be a learning process. What's more, it is probably the best way to arrive at your Top Dollar asking price. And yet, even after obtaining all this information, you may make an additional adjustment in that price, either upward or downward, based on further suggestions and guidelines found throughout this book.

Remember too that the area of the country in which your home is located may also have a bearing on that price adjustment. For instance, in 1979, the average single-family home in the United States sold for $69,000. However, in some areas of the Sun Belt States—and especially in California—that average price exceeded $110,000. Thus, if you have any question whether your home is situated within one of these fast-growing sections of the country, be sure to ask the professionals if they may have considered that factor while formulating their appraisal price.

But the final decision—and responsibility—for that asking price is up to you. What's more, if you feel that there is something uniquely special about your home (and nearly every home is special in some way), then don't be afraid to add a little to the price the experts suggest to you. After all, our judgment is not faultless. We can be wrong too.

Why, I remember one couple who had bought a rather nice

Colonial home through my office about ten years earlier for some $21,000. They had made a few improvements, but now, because the children were all in school, the place was just too large for them. So they invited me over one Saturday morning to discuss listing it. About half way through our second cup of coffee, though, they sprang the question: What do you think we should sell it for? Well, considering what they paid for the home, what improvements they had made, and what comparable homes in the area were being listed at, I gallantly replied, "Oh, we shouldn't have any trouble getting around $60,000 for it."

There was a dead silence. The loving, warm expressions that only moments earlier had graced their faces quickly vanished. "Oh, no," they finally blurted out, "we feel this is a very special home, and we couldn't consider taking a nickel less than $75,000 for it."

"Okay, you can try to get that much," I said. "But as a friend I've got to tell you that's about $15,000 too much. I'll take the key, but I know it's not going to sell." And this time, for some reason, I added, "But if it does, if you get anything over $70,000, then I'll take you two out for the most lavish French dinner around." They were so confident that they countered with the same offer, should the house sell for less than $70,000.

We shook hands on the deal; I returned home to save my appetite for some fine French food and nearly forgot about the entire episode until about three months later, when the couple appeared one day in my office and asked, "Well, when are we going to dinner?" As it turned out, they not only had sold their home but had gotten only a little less than $75,000 to boot. Incidentally I did enjoy that dinner, and the lesson I learned was certainly good food for thought.

Now that doesn't happen too often. But when it does it teaches us two things: that even the most knowledgeable of people can be wrong—this time I was wrong to the tune of nearly

$15,000—and, more important, that the Top Dollar price for your home boils down to what a willing buyer will pay for it. It's as simple as that.

# 3

## *Is This the Best Time to Sell?*

Now I realize that, for most people, the sale of a home involves little, if any, element of choice. Maybe you've outgrown your present home, or maybe it's become too large or expensive to maintain. Or perhaps you've been transferred to another community or simply want to retire to a warm climate. In any of these situations, there is, as I say, little choice. You put your home on the market, and you hope for the best.

However, for those of you who are still on the fence regarding that sale, let me offer just one piece of advice: Don't rush into anything. Consider all the socioeconomic factors I have listed below *before* making your decision. Who knows, if you don't have to sell today, it may pay, for one reason or another, for you to hang on to that home for a while.

For example, I am reminded of the fifty-year-old pharmacist and his wife who, a year or so ago, came to ask me to list their good-size, five-bedroom home in a fashionable section of town. Again, they no longer needed all that much space, and, figuring what with the smaller families and larger heating bills today few others would either, they thought they'd better sell it at a profit while they still could. However, I knew that a major production plant was soon to be built on the outskirts of town and that, within a year or so, there would at least be a couple of high-income executives, with large families, who could afford such a home—and perhaps even pay more than their $90,000 asking price. After all, considering new construction costs even then, it would take about $140,000 to duplicate it.

But, no, the man didn't want to take that "risk." So we sold his home, nearly overnight, for his asking price, and, as I predicted, within a year the few homes of similar size placed on the market brought as much as $125,000. The lesson: Sometimes there is information that makes it obvious that this is not the best time to sell. When this is true, you should certainly take another long look at your decision to sell.

On the other hand, don't base that decision not to sell now on some pipe dream reason, thinking perhaps that maybe a plant will move into the area. Indeed, for those of you in a should-I-or-shouldn't-I position, there is enough information—area economic conditions, availability of financing, market supply and demand, not to mention national and international trends —on which to base your decision. And even then, you are only predicting the future.

Sure, I admit it is a difficult decision to make. Just look at the record: During the last decade the pendulum between abundant prosperity and so-called recession has swung in rather unpredictable and erratic cycles. Thus, the time frame governing when to sell and when not to has been of shorter duration too, especially in contrast to the historically more extended periods of depression and recovery. Now add to this the fact that you may have economic growth in one area of the country and not in another, and you'll realize that owning a home in the right place at the right time is a combination of circumstance and luck, in addition to the many other contributing factors that will help you decide whether to "sell" or "hold." In fact, before making any decision review these positive—and negative—indicators regarding the sale of a home today.

### Positive Indicators

- The cost of land and land development for housing purposes, coupled with environmental restrictions, will curtail the building of new homes, thus increasing the demand for existing homes.
- Changing life-styles, a rising divorce rate, and smaller families have contributed to a tremendous demand for the smaller living unit, as opposed to the larger-type single home. Every indication points to this trend continuing—a benefit to the owner of a smaller home.
- Investors in great numbers are turning to single-family-home purchases and converting them to rentals. Larger homes, adaptable for conversion to more than one unit or professional offices (zoning laws permitting), are attracting greater interest due to the high cost of new construction.
- Most communities throughout the country offer special property-tax abatements to senior citizens, who have turned away from escalating rentals and are now looking for more space and comfort, and acceptable living quarters.
- Alternative sources of energy, easily installed in private homes (and carrying with them income tax breaks), are lowering the high cost of heating and cooling residences.
- Billions of dollars in federal and state subsidies are anticipated for public transportation systems, thus affording high-income city workers an opportunity to live in the suburbs or country at a lower cost than that of present city accommodations.
- With continuing inflation and higher personal incomes, the demand for single-family homes will increase, providing that tax laws permit the deduction of interest on mortgages and property taxes.
- The alarming deterioration of public school systems in major

cities and the prohibitive cost of city private schools will offer no other alternative to many families than to purchase homes in suburban or country areas with good public school systems.

- "Pump priming"—always associated with national or local elections, will provide large sums of money in the mortgage market in an effort to stimulate home-buying activity.
- Great numbers of foreigners look to the United States as the world's most stable economy and government. If the present trend continues, hundreds of thousands of homes will be purchased directly and indirectly by people from other countries either as permanent residences or as a haven from the troubles of the world. A $100,000 American home represents to many foreigners only a $50,000 investment, under attractive monetary exchange rates.

### Negative Indicators

- Our economy is rapidly approaching the point where a large segment of the home-buying public simply cannot afford to build, buy, or maintain a home.
- The cost and method of institutional home financing are undergoing radical, negative changes that can only reduce the home-buying stampede of the past ten years.
- Investors no longer find it financially attractive to build apartment complexes—in fact, the trend is toward rapid conversion of rental apartments to condominiums and cooperatives. Most apartment dwellers have responded favorably to the conversions, not only because the offering prices have been attractive, but because alternatives in housing accommodations at comparable costs are limited.
- As increasing numbers of women enter the work force and have less time for homemaking, tangible interest in the single-family home is substantially reduced. Compounding this attitude is the critical shortage of domestic help.

- Interest in the large, luxury homes and estates, although attractively priced, is dwindling, primarily due to the high cost of maintenance, ever-increasing property taxes, problems in staffing, and a trend away from formal living.
- Indicators of population growth are negative. Homes located in states that are experiencing major downward population shifts are not commanding Top Dollar, as the supply exceeds demand.
- Homeowners on fixed, limited incomes are finding it more and more difficult to meet the cost of major improvements.
- Some economic barometers indicate a mild to deep recession for the early eighties. New housing construction and auto production, both vital to a healthy economy, are sluggish.
- Worldwide unrest, creating havoc with our general economy, could lead to international economic depression.
- The energy crisis and all costs relating thereto are bound to have some negative repercussions in the second-home market.

Sure, every generation has lived through "troubled times." Obviously, ours is no exception. However, today there are safeguards to prevent another 1929-type crash. What's more, for most of you, your home has been increasing in value despite most economic conditions. Why, in the last decade alone, most residences have nearly doubled in value—and that trend is expected to continue well into the 1980s. (Some say that by 1990 there will be a demand for some fifteen million new households.) Then again, take a look at what has happened to gold. Not that long ago, few would have predicted the price would ever go above $100 an ounce. My point here is: How high is high? Or, what is Top Dollar today *may be* even higher tomorrow.

But for those of you who are born pessimists and don't have to sell but want to, cash in your Top Dollar chips today and enjoy the trip to the bank.

# 4

# *Getting Your Act Together*

When it comes to selling a home today, the old expression "putting your house in order" means a lot more than straightening the sofa pillows. In this paper-chase society of ours, it has become a complicated procedure to say the least. In fact, it might be compared to one of those nerve-racking giant jigsaw puzzles. But, in this case, the homeowner is not only responsible for making all the pieces fit; he or she must also find all the pieces to begin with!

What? You say that when you bought your home, thirty years ago, you didn't need all the paper work required to sell it today. No, of course not. We were living in much simpler times then. But now, if you plan to sell, you're surrounded by an entourage of FBI types demanding enough documentation to fill the Library of Congress—or at least it seems that way.

Actually the demands made by your attorney and your realtor/broker are not all that unreasonable. Indeed, they are made in order to protect *you*. After all, we are living in what seems to be a "law-suit happy" society, and far too often I have seen problems that arise over the sale of a home wind up in court. Remember that any representation made by you or your agent pertaining to size of plot or acreage, cost of utilities, zoning, water and sewage (if not public), property taxes, insurance costs, easements and right of way of others, or the specific physical condition of *anything* must be thoroughly documented. In other words, if, after the closing, your buyer discovers that half of the garage you said you owned is located on your former neighbor's property, don't be surprised when you're served with a law suit.

Take my word for it, the days are gone when a little boasting on the part of the homeowner or a bit of exaggeration from the real estate agent was expected and taken for granted by a prospective buyer. What was then "five acres, more or less," by legal deed is now 4.97 or 5.32 acres on the certified survey that is guaranteed by the title company and recorded in the county clerk's office. Indeed, most roadblocks to a swift and smooth closing today concern some conflict over acreage, water supply, or so-called clean title to the property. And again believe me, these legal snags can be frustrating and costly—and they can also result in the loss of your buyer.

But even that isn't as bad as what happened to one home seller who came to me not ago for help. A middle-aged, now-successful artist had bought his present home some twenty-five years earlier, upon graduating from college. The purchase price was comparatively low then, and the owners had cooperated by taking back a ten-year mortgage at a low interest rate. Yet, throughout that period, even during those beginning years when the man struggled at his craft, he made his payments promptly and, on his final check, wrote "paid in full." Well, that was what he thought. Everyone was happy, everyone, that is, except his attorney who, all those years later, when the house was sold, couldn't find a simple little form known as a satisfaction of mortgage anywhere on record.

Of course, the artist had not known that one was necessary,

so now he came to me with his problem. Having been in the area for a good number of years, I—and my assistants—were finally able to locate the previous owners alive and well—and living somewhere on the outskirts of Lima, Peru!

In the meantime, however, the time limit on the man's contract of sale had expired. Fortunately the lawyer, aware of the peculiar situation and terribly understanding, agreed to extend it another thirty days. Again it seemed that everyone was pleased: The artist had received a sum close to his $95,000 Top Dollar asking price, we had engineered the sale and the financing (no easy trick today), and the lawyers knew the mortgage satisfaction was on its way. But, only three days before that letter arrived, the man's house burned to the ground—and, to make matters worse, he had failed throughout the years to update the value of his home on his insurance policy (another document) and thus received far less than $50,000 in final settlement.

So let this unfortunate fellow be a lesson to you. Whether you plan to sell your home in the immediate future or not, you must get your portfolio together and make certain that it is as up-to-date as possible. In fact, before you even call in an attorney or a realtor/broker, you should purchase a dozen or so file folders, or one of those accordian-type folders with all the compartments, and begin assembling the following documents, legal papers, and receipts necessary for a successful closing.

*Deed or Deeds to the Property:* The deed to your home is the legal instrument you received at the time of purchase. It will probably be in one of four places: your bank safe deposit box; the office of the lawyer who represented you at the closing; the kitchen drawer third from the top, where you keep all important papers, such as the telephone book and old paid bills; or the tin box underneath the neckties in your bureau drawer. If it is not in any of these places, your county clerk or other recording office will prepare photostatic copies upon request for a small fee.

If you have acquired additional property that you intend to

offer for sale, or have sold any portion of your original purchase, it is important to obtain copies of these transfers and attach them to the original deed.

It is likely you do not have a deed to your home if you are purchasing under contract and have not completed full payment. In some areas it is common practice to have the deed held "in trust" until the property is fully paid for, or until the mortgage held by the seller at the time of purchase has been satisfied. In this case, however, the legal description of the property should be attached to the contract of purchase.

The primary purpose in finding your deed is not for the value of the legal document itself, but to obtain a legal description of the property you are selling. One can only sell exactly what one owns; no more, no less. The deed will also refresh your memory as to other salient restrictions and rights applicable to yourself and others. Certain restrictions must be adhered to by all future owners, and some of those restrictions may be a deterrent to a prospective buyer once they are known. You might have forgotten that you bought the property subject to the right of a neighbor to use your driveway to get to his property. And this easement is still in effect, whether the neighbor takes advantage of it or not. Or reading the deed might remind you that your property cannot be offered for sale until the previous owner has exercised a right to buy it back or, worse yet, to buy it back at a price lower than that you are offering the general public.

In addition, local zoning ordinances might allow limited commercial or professional use, but *your* deed may limit such use to "residential purposes only." The deed will also remind you whether any changes in ownership have been updated on record. Several years ago you might have deeded all or part to a member of your family, and the title now rests with others than those stated in the deed at hand. Reading further, you might even find only a vague description of your property, indicating that you bought it without benefit of a formal survey.

These are but a few examples of the information you can learn from your deed. Before offering your home for sale, you must determine the answers to these deed questions:

- Can you or your attorney specifically describe the property you plan to sell?
- Do you know the boundaries and exact size of the plot or acreage?
- Are you familiar with all restrictions and easements (other's rights to the property, including mineral, water, and drilling) legally binding all future owners?
- Do you have specific and legal descriptions of any property acquired or sold from your original purchase?
- Do you have pertinent details in legal form of any rights granted to public utility companies and the like during the period of your ownership?

If the answer to any of the above is "I am not absolutely sure," "I don't know," or, "I think so," then note these items for future discussion with your attorney. Meanwhile, the next section will provide some of the answers to the above questions.

*Surveys, Survey Maps, Tax Maps:* To those of you who had a surveyor or professional engineer survey your property prior to acquisition—congratulations! Just locate the map and place it in your file. Even if you've lost it, your local or county recording office will probably have a copy and will be willing to photostat several more copies at a nominal fee. If the map was not recorded, check with the surveying office for copies. (Note: Assuming your home was acquired by survey description, the deed will usually make reference to the surveyor, date, book, and page where recorded.)

If you live in an urban community or well-developed suburban area, it is likely a formal mapping has been done and is recorded with local authorities. If so, obtain several copies of your specific parcel and place them in your file. On the other hand, if you live in a smaller hamlet or village in a rural or semirural area, your county or township may have undertaken a tax-mapping program, even having on file a reasonable description of each parcel within its boundaries, but do not confuse these maps with an accurate survey. They only represent reasonable estimates, unless they were prepared by licensed engineers or surveyors on a county-wide or similar basis.

"But why should I have a survey made now?" you may well ask. "I bought the place without one and have lived here twenty years without a problem. And maybe the buyer won't insist on having one either. Or, if he does, let him pay for at least a part of it."

To answer your argument, I can only say that a substantial number of banking institutions *require* an updated survey certified to the title insurance company by a licensed surveyor or engineer prior to granting a mortgage. In addition, buyers and their attorneys will insist on knowing every blade of grass surrounding your home, and, with the cost of each blade today, you cannot blame them. Gone are the days when transferring a parcel of land with a house on it was a rather nonchalant process, when "more or less" meant exactly that. Today many courts have ruled that "more or less" allows for no more than a 5 percent variation. In other words, if a buyer purchases your "fifty" unsurveyed acres and decides a year after closing to have the property surveyed, he may discover that the fifty acres are really only forty, and you, your real estate agent, and everyone else involved are looking at a law suit. Furthermore, a check of court records reveals most litigation in real estate cases could have been avoided if the buyer and seller knew, without any doubt, exactly what they were buying or selling. (Remember, though, that most sellers do not *willfully* misrepresent their property. They're only relying on those vague deed descriptions and representations of previous owners who more than likely also relied on vague deed descriptions and representations.) Regardless, however, more than three-fourths of all problems in closing sales of homes with some acreage stem from a lack of a formal survey.

Keep in mind, too, if your property has substantial public road frontage (more than 1,000 feet), a portion of that frontage is now automatically owned by the state, county, or highway department by virtue of statutes recently passed in many states. In this case, an updated survey may show a reduced amount of saleable acreage, which, in turn, may result in a reduced sale price, litigation, or no deal at all.

It is not all that uncommon, on the other hand, to discover, once the survey is completed, that you own *more* land than you thought. But even this may be a problem, for it's not always easy, for example, to explain to your neighbor that their rose garden actually belongs to you!

It is not sufficient, either, that a survey reveal only a boundary description of your property. It must also show the location of all buildings on it, drawn to scale. And the problem today is not only the cost of such a survey, it's coping with the shortage of licensed surveyors and land engineers—then coping with severe weather conditions that can often hinder their work. If you're having difficulty finding a qualified surveyor, ask your attorney or bankers to recommend at least a couple of individuals or firms in your area. Get them to submit estimates, and get it done.

Now, even if you did have a complete survey done when you bought your property, and no additions or subtractions have taken place, most buyers, attorneys, and title companies will still ask for a recertification of that survey, updated to the day of closing. So you might as well do this *in advance* of listing your home and avoid any problems that might occur later on. (For instance, you might discover that the original surveyor was not licensed, so now you're back to point zero.) Now, thoroughly examine this updated survey to see if it coincides with your knowledge of the property. And make certain the surveyor's name, license number, and seal appear somewhere. This information alone will make the difference between a map of authority—and just a map.

*Title Insurance Policy or Title Search:* Depending upon when you bought your home, and upon procedures which vary in different parts of the country, there should also be in your possession one of two things: either a title insurance policy issued by the title insurance company, or a rather thick document known as a title search, prepared by the attorney representing you at the time of purchase.

The title policy guaranteed you marketable title with the insurance company's blessing for as long as you owned your home. The title search was guaranteed by the attorney representing you. And together these documents established that, at the time of purchase, your home was free and clear of all liens, judgments, mortgages, and unpaid taxes. Today they will guarantee a much smoother closing.

*Property Taxes:* Place in your file a copy of your property tax bills for the past year. This should include land, school, water, refuse collection, specific assessments, *etc.* If you have lost any or all of these, ask your appropriate tax collector or treasurer for a letter detailing these charges, or for copies of the bills. It is suggested you contact the chairman of each local taxing authority for an opinion about any major increase or decrease in the present taxes assessed against your property, and so inform the buyer.

Buyers frequently ask about property assessment. More often than not, this figure does not reflect the real market value or asking price of the property unless a recent reappraisal was instituted by the taxing authorities in your community. Various state legislatures have enacted laws in an effort to program all property taxes at 100 percent of market value. The goal of this mandate is to make uniform the assessment process on a more equitable basis. Thus, in the event your property is not assessed at current market value, familiarize yourself with the present basis of assessment and advise your prospective buyers or their agents accordingly. In any case, I strongly caution against making any boastful claims of "low" taxes. If you live in a community where tax assessments are as antiquated as the horse and buggy, the moment your property transfers to a new owner its taxes may double or triple, based on the new sale price. And this is another reason why law suits claiming misrepresentation have also doubled and tripled!

On the other hand, let us assume that your property taxes are especially high now (at least in your opinion) and out of proportion to comparable properties. Now certainly is the time to take whatever action possible to get them reduced, for property taxes are a Top Dollar factor in the buying/selling process.

*Mortgage:* Most likely you have a mortgage balance due. If so, a copy of the mortgage should be made part of this portfolio of information. If you have misplaced your copy, call your banking institution or lender and ask for another. Obtain a current statement from the lender of balance due, the monthly payments of principal and interest, and any other additional payments for taxes and insurance. Determine how many more months or years are left before the mortgage is paid in full. Ask the mortgage officer if you are permitted to prepay without penalty and under what conditions a prospective purchaser might assume your mortgage. A letter from the lending institution incorporating this data will come in very handy.

*Insurance:* All insurance policies for fire, theft, liability, or special coverage, plus a memo of costs, should be an integral part of this file. Indeed, this might be a good time for you and your agent to possibly increase your present coverage for two reasons: first, to protect your investment, and, second, to save you the embarrassment of having a prospective buyer ask, "Why, when your asking price is $140,000, do you only carry $100,000 worth of insurance?" Some insurance companies are reluctant, however, to extend the amount of coverage requested by the homeowner, even though the purchase price equals or exceeds the amount applied for. Should you find yourself in this dilemma, check with other companies for additional coverage. If you cannot receive it, obtain a letter for your file stating these facts.

If you have not done so, this might be an appropriate time to consolidate all coverage regarding your home into a package-type insurance known as an all-inclusive homeowner's policy. Consideration should also be given to obtaining a couple of estimates for all coverage in an attempt to broaden it and at the same time reduce your costs. Then, too, consult with various agents for a review of improvements you might consider making which would reduce premium costs, such as updating of electrical wiring or installation of fire and smoke alarm systems, fire extinguishers, or burglar alarms.

*Engineering or Contractor Inspection Report:* In many parts of the country, particularly in heavily populated areas, it is becoming routine procedure for the buyer to hire an inspector to investigate the overall condition of the property. However, you should beat them to it by doing it yourself. Now, although these reports cost an average of $300, it is a good investment. Why? Because as a seller you can foresee—and correct—any condition that may result in a lowering of your Top Dollar price—or the loss of a sale. Then, too, it serves as a major step toward gaining the confidence of a prospective buyer.

*Guarantee and Warranties:* Add to your file unexpired warranties on such things as new roofing, heating systems, appliances, service contracts, swimming pool systems, and the like. These guarantees are reassuring to a new buyer and definitely contribute to the value of your home.

*Contracts and Leases:* Leases for occupancy by others for *any* portion of your property or land for *any* reason should be reviewed and placed in the file. This is of special importance if the obligation to your tenant or tenants does not cease with the sale of the property. Likewise open contracts for work in process, or that yet to be performed, will also have to be resolved or brought to the attention of the new buyer.

*Utility Bills:* Locate your last twelve months' utility bills, if readily available, and put them in the file. Buyers are placing particular emphasis on the *quantity* of fuel consumed and not just the cost, what with continuing increases in the price of oil and gas. Be sure to tell the buyer if your home was not occupied for any part of the year. As an alternative to locating the bills, call your local public-service utility or oil company and ask for a letter stating the number of units consumed. The letter should also state expectation of cost for the upcoming twelve months, using the previous year as a basis of consumption.

*Miscellaneous:* It is helpful to have any photographs or architectural drawings of the improvements that have been made to your home during the years.

A sketch, map, or diagram showing the location of your water and sewage lines, wells, and septic tanks, is also a plus. Try to obtain a document from the original installer or engineer listing the depth of the well, gallons-per-minute flow, and the size of your sewage disposal system. You may not have been given all this information when you bought the home, but chances are ninety-nine out of one hundred you are not going to sell the property until this information is available.

If your home is not served with public water, call your local health department to obtain a water-sample test for its potability. (If your health department does not provide this service, contact a private, licensed laboratory or water engineer.) Do it now, and place results, if favorable, in your file. If the test is unfavorable, that means you've been drinking polluted water for who knows how long, so get the situation corrected before the buyer becomes involved, even if it means drilling another well.

If you are serving as an agent, not as owner, of an estate or for a partnership, corporation, trust, or some other entity, there will be additional legal papers you will need to make available. These might include the copies of a will, your authorization as agent, certified proof of payment of various federal, state, local property, and estate taxes, resolutions, and releases.

And, finally, you may want to prepare a list including the name, address, and phone number of all those individuals who know your property well and who you would recommend to a new buyer: that is, the plumber, electrician, pump man, roofer, gardener, chimney sweep, butcher, baker, and candlestick maker. You'd be surprised how much a seemingly unimportant listing such as this may one day help you achieve your asking price.

All of these documents, viewed as a collection, represent necessary homework if you want to achieve Top Dollar results. That's why, once you've got your files complete, you should make several photocopies of each item, one for the buyer and his attorney, one for your attorney, one for the real estate agent, and perhaps one for the appraiser. And be careful to include all the items I've mentioned because one missing link in this long chain of paper can make the difference between a pleasant, profitable, and peaceful closing—and no closing at all.

# 5

## *Over 100 Low-Cost Improvements That Turn Buyers On*

Once a home is acquired, the motivations for improvements are an immediate need for space, comfort, and convenience, and a sense of pride. Consideration is seldom given to whether these improvements will increase the resale value of the property. Justification for the above-average, luxury-labeled projects, such as tennis courts, indoor swimming pools, pebbled patios, elaborate built-in hi-fi systems, sliding glass doors leading to more sliding glass doors is: "It's strictly an investment and will be added to the price of the home when it is sold." This may be true in the Hollywood Hills, but not in the heartland of practical America.

You will be well rewarded for the time, effort, and funds expended on the following improvements, which will be meaningful to most would-be home owners. Property improvements are limitless, but there is a point of no return.

### *Inside—Under $100*

- Wash all windows inside and out.

- Remove every bit of grease from the inside of the oven or ovens.
- Get all the bugs and flies out of all light fixtures.
- If you can't get rid of the stains in the toilet bowl, buy a new one. This applies to all bathrooms, including the one in the cellar that doesn't work.
- Put a 100-watt bulb in all stairwell fixtures.
- Send all cats, dogs, parrots, hamsters, and pet monkeys to your brother-in-law from the day the house goes on the market until the day it is sold, and get rid of the odors that are left behind. Over 50 percent of home purchasers are either allergic to or afraid of, or simply dislike animals.
- Clean all the rubbish out of all fireplaces, particularly the ones you haven't lit in the last three years.
- Put two coats of off-white paint over the chartreuse- and tangerine-striped walls of the back bedroom.
- Open all the drapes, pull up the shades, and let the light in.
- Fix the front door bell.
- Shampoo the carpets or carpeting.
- Put new washers in all the dripping faucets.
- Throw away the torn shower curtain and put up a new one.
- Remove junk from the attic, cellar, hall closet, and toolshed, and have a successful garage sale. Contribute whatever remains to the next garbage pickup.
- Turn off all blaring phonographs, stereos, and TV sets while the house is being shown.
- Water all dying plants or get rid of them.
- Adjust all doors and windows so they can be opened and closed without causing a double hernia.
- Dust, clean, scrub everything—that means *everything*—from attic to cellar.
- Replace broken tiles on walls or floors.
- Repaste loose or dangling wallpaper.
- Make the beds or strip them.

- Send the dishes in the sink to Parke Bernet if they have been there long enough to become collector's items.
- Secure all banisters and handrails.
- Organize all closets.
- Smile.

You might have chuckled or frowned after reading the above list. Trivial as they may seem, these "little things that mean a lot" might be the difference between turning on and turning off the buyer you have been waiting for.

### Outside—Under $100

- Rake the leaves and mow the lawn.
- Fill the potholes in the driveway.
- Fix the garage door so it opens and closes.
- Remove the dead trees, plants, bushes, and shrubs—trim and cultivate the live ones.
- Straighten the leaning TV antenna.
- Attach the downspouts to the gutters.
- Paint the front, back, and side entrance doors. Nothing looks worse than a peeling door.
- Tack the broken shutters.
- Nail down the three loose shingles or tiles on the roof.
- Clean the inside of the pool and fill the obvious cracks.
- Buy a new mailbox without graffiti on it.
- The fence is falling, and so is the sale. Get rid of it or replace it.
- Clean the outdoor barbecue.
- Put some crushed stone on walkways that turn muddy in the rain.
- Put scattered garbage cans behind the garage or out of sight.
- Remove old lawn mowers, tractors, disabled autos, broken lawn ornaments, topless tables, armless lawn furniture, and seatless chairs. They are reasons for a buyer to make a U-turn.

- Shovel snow from the driveway, paths, and front walk. Melt the ice.
- Weed and cultivate the home-garden area. If you have no garden, prepare an adequate site for potential gardeners.
- Plant a good variety of annuals and perennials, weather and area permitting.
- Clean all outdoor buildings, sheds, kennels, and garages.
- Remove the half-dozen, slightly tilted, multicolored "For Sale" signs.

### *Inside—Over $100*

- Make all basic energy-saving improvements, particularly those that provide maximum home insulation—weather stripping, storm windows, and the like. Update all heating systems to maximum efficiency.
- Install a wood-burning stove or fireplace for both practical and romantic appeal.
- Install an additional half or full bath in homes with only one bathroom.
- Modernize or improve the kitchen with particular emphasis on cabinet space, seating capacity, natural light, and built-in appliances, especially the stove and dishwasher.
- Eliminate the maze of fuse boxes in the cellar and consolidate them into a modern circuit-breaker panel. It is important to have a minimum of 200-amp service coming in for distribution.
- Paint the cellar floor and whitewash the cellar walls.
- Install a sump pump and exterior and interior drains if the cellar has a tendency to flood or is subject to water seepage.
- Touch up with paint any areas that are obviously in need. The choice of colors should be neutral, preferably off-white.
- Plaster, replace, or cover with Sheetrock (not plywood paneling or commercial blocks) walls and ceilings that show major cracks or damage.

- Suspended block ceilings cover a multitude of sins and are inexpensive to install. They do not appeal to most sophisticated buyers, however.
- Improve the plumbing system and piping to increase water pressure throughout your home.
- Remove worn out wall-to-wall carpeting, providing base floors are either hardwood, wide board (in fairly good condition), or tile. Buff and clean the floors.
- Provide additional closet space wherever possible if adequate storage is lacking.
- Remove excess extension cords and exposed wires to lamps and fixtures, and replace them with permanent outlets.
- If the cost is not excessive, restore the architectural integrity of any portion of your home. An example of this is removing paint from exposed beams, fireplace mantels, doors and moldings, or fine hardware.
- Install washer/dryer facilities with proper outlets either in or adjacent to the kitchen, if presently nonexistent or in hard-to-reach cellar.
- Install a minimum number of air-conditioning units, particularly if you live in a warm climate zone.
- Have your home inspected by a reliable firm specializing in termite and other pest-infestation control prior to offering it for sale. If a problem exists, have it corrected and obtain a certificate that states your home is problem-free.
- Replace all broken screens, cracked window panes, faulty light fixtures, loose cellar-stair steps, or anything else not in good working condition.
- Convert to year-round use any room, enclosed porch, or breezeway by installing insulation, proper windows, and heating. If extension of heat from the central system is not practical or too costly, a few individual electric heating units might solve the problem.

*Outside—Over $100*

- If your home is close to a busy street or highway, a tall hedge or fast-growing row of trees will provide a sense of privacy and reduce noise. This is also applicable for screening out any environmental negatives within sight of your property. If time is of the essence, high fencing is an alternative. Anything is better than looking at the rear of a junk-car lot or watching the local drag racers speed by the front door.
- Make a provision for one or two cars. This may be accomplished by a garage or a carport, depending on general climate conditions.
- Repair or replace broken sidewalks and driveways.
- Provide a maximum amount of "green" for aesthetic effect, shade, and landscaping purposes, but do not create a jungle.
- If you are neither prepared to nor wish to spend thousands of dollars for exterior painting, be ready either to make an immediate price adjustment, or listen to everyone who views the home say, "It will cost a fortune to have the house painted!" If you can afford it, the money spent tidying up will be well worth the investment.
- I do not recommend covering good clapboard siding, particularly on an older home. Let the new buyer do so, if that's his preference.
- Replace defective gutters, leaders, and hole-ridden eaves.
- Point all chimneys and replace broken brick or stone. If the roof is slate or tile, replace broken or missing units.
- Remove any overhanging branches from the roof and clean away accumulated moss.
- If the roof leaks, fix it! Remove any or all evidence of leakage by whatever means possible. If the roof is beyond reasonable repair, call the home improvement manager at your friendly local bank.

- Any major or minor defects in the foundation demand your immediate attention.
- Have the TV repairman replace support wires that are blowing in the wind.
- Stone walls lining the entrance to the driveway score 9.9 on a scale of 1 to 10—but not if most of the stones are strewn about in the poison ivy and overgrown sumac.
- Now is the time to call your local federal or state conservation department for procedures to rid the stream or pond of its three-inch accumulation of algae. Any watershed area enhances the value of the property.
- Replace or repair all broken steps, front, back, and side.
- Installation of an outside spotlight or security lights to illuminate a reasonable area surrounding the primary home is a practical recommendation—realtors make many appointments in the evening.
- Most buyers appreciate automatic garage door openers—not absolutely necessary, but they make a good impression.
- The most modest circular driveway is a major plus. Those who have them very rarely use them, but they do have a magnetic attraction for buyers.
- If you are fortunate enough to live where there are birds, place a few substantial bird feeders in a permanent position within view of frequently used rooms. They serve as automatic pacifiers for neurotic buyers, and they are also great for the birds.
- Build a woodshed and stock it with a few cords of wood.
- Whatever it takes to bring more natural light into the home, do it!

Preparing a home for sale should begin the day after it is purchased. An overall misconception held by great numbers of homeowners is that when the time comes to sell it they will be able to recoup every investment they make inside and outside their homes. For those of you who are anticipating selling your home in the near future, there are improvements that will not only expedite the sale, but will actually increase the value of your home, without your spending a great deal of money. On the other side of the coin, be careful not to spend thousands of dollars, overqualify the property, and lose a bundle.

# II

# *Making the Sale Fly*

# 6

## *Finding the Indispensable Broker/Realtor*

It is not turning the screw that matters—it's knowing what screw to turn. There are about 800,000 licensed real estate brokers in the United States who sell millions of homes each year. For the most part, the results are good. Shooting for Top Dollar means selecting the best real estate professional, one with a proven track record of performance, the highest level of integrity, unique and aggressive marketing techniques, and an abundance of enthusiasm and optimism. Similar to most professional services, there are many real estate people at the top. Yet if you are going to extend one the privilege of selling your home—and it is, indeed, a privilege—this chapter should help establish some priorities and guidelines for doing so.

In today's market it is more important than ever before to find the right broker/realtor for your home sale. You must find the individual, or firm of individuals, who are most creative and imaginative in their marketing techniques and innovative in their solution to the financial dilemma in this tight money market. And yet you needn't be a J.P. Morgan-type financial wizard to ask a few leading questions—and understand the answers.

As you interview realtors, ask them what thoughts they have pertaining to the financing of your home. And listen for answers in addition to your taking back a mortgage. Also ask them about their relationship with the local banks. Have their experiences with a good number of mortgage lending institutions been extensive? And, last, ask them if they would be willing to take back part of their commission in the form of a mortgage or short-term, low-interest loan, or if they have a special fund set aside to do so. Believe me, it's happening every day, mainly because most brokers realize that half a loaf is better than none (although, in time, they do get the entire loaf). Then, too, it sure beats being asked to cut the commission.

As you can see, there's a lot more to selecting a broker than settling on cousin George down the street. You've got to find the one who has a financial plan in mind and, in addition, one who is well known for handling your type of property.

The average real estate office in the typical American community handles a variety of properties in both residential and commercial classifications. But the majority of its sales are of residential properties. Some firms specialize in homes within various price ranges or limit most of their activity to a specific area or neighborhood. There is a trend within the real estate profession toward specialization of property and price ranges.

Real estate sales have more than their share of flukes. Often, a property is sold for close to the asking price by a one-person agency after the so-called "hot shots" have made their best effort and failed. Although the law of averages does not deal with the exception, when it comes to selling a home, strange things do happen.

The personality and attitude of the selling broker are the key ingredients to consider, if your relationship is to be successful. Interviewing several real estate people prior to making any commitment is recommended. Contact local bankers and attorneys for their opinions of those realtors/brokers whom they feel are most competent to sell your particular home. For further advice and counsel, check with people you know who recently sold their homes.

Now that you have narrowed your list to five or six brokers, make an appointment with the principal of the firm or agency to come to your home and present to you a proposal composed of the following:

- Suggested asking price justification
- Commission or fee to be charged
- Term and type of listing
- Marketing techniques proposed
- Honest opinion of home sale potential
- Suggestions for improving marketability
- Descriptions of last five properties sold in comparable price range
- A statement of relationship with financing institutions extending mortgages
- Reasons why *they* think *they* can sell it.

This consultation with the broker's representative is a valuable learning process and should be a listening one as well. Refrain from injecting your personal opinions, particularly in the asking-price category. Request from each office a letter which puts in writing the formal proposal of listing, as well as a copy of their listing-agreement form. Naturally, you will be most favorably impressed with those quoting the highest suggested asking prices. However, that is only *one* of several important factors to be considered.

The homeowner must be extremely careful to avoid creating an unintended legal obligation between himself and an agent, an obligation which is enforceable under many state laws even though it is *not* in writing! Creation of an agency relationship may become legal by oral, inferred, or written agreement.

Therefore, a nonchalant listing of your home could result in an obligation to pay commission to a licensed broker who procures a buyer ready, willing and able to purchase. Under *no* circumstances should you become involved with any listing agreement, whether oral or in writing, without first consulting with your attorney. True, this is not the procedure usually followed —but that is why every court calendar has its share of litigations involving claims for real estate commissions.

There are four basic types of listings:

*Open Listing:* The seller has the right to retain as many brokers to act as agent as he or she wishes. The seller also may sell the property himself without any obligation to pay anyone a commission, providing the buyer had no involvement with any open-listing brokers.

*Exclusive Agency:* Under this type of listing, only one broker may act on behalf of the seller. The seller retains the right to sell the property himself without any obligation for commission to the exclusive broker, providing the broker was not involved in procuring the buyer.

*Exclusive Right to Sell:* One broker is appointed as the sole agent of the seller, with absolute and exclusive right to sell the home. The seller will be obligated to pay a commission to the broker even if the seller generates the customer and is responsible for the sale of the home.

*Multiple Listing:* This is the same as the exclusive right to sell with the exception that the exclusive broker is given the additional right to distribute the listing to all brokers who are members of a multiple-listing organization. The seller is obligated to pay the listing broker the agreed commission. The broker, in turn, shares that commission with the member of the multiple-listing organization who is responsible for the sale of the exclusive listing. The mechanics of multiple listing vary throughout the country, but the basic concept is the same.

There are advantages and disadvantages to the seller with

each type of listing. The seller of a home can become totally confused with this maze of choices. It all comes down to one principle—the greater number of qualified buyers generated by the listing broker or brokers, the sooner the home will be sold at Top Dollar. Therefore, it would appear that the open listing, with any number of reliable brokers, would bring the best results. Competition has always been known to be a good stimulant to activity, and this arrangement throws the door open so competitive juices may flow. Major brokerage firms reject the open-listing opportunity, however, because they are reluctant to spend a lot of money on advertising a listing without having any control over potential purchasers. There is a further reluctance to become involved in an open listing due to the time required in working with one client to obtain financing and other necessary arrangements before the contract is signed. It is during this crucial period that some other broker might step in and sell the property out from under the first.

The exclusive-agency listing limits the seller to the exposure and efforts of one agency. Therefore, if a homeowner enters into this type of agreement, the exclusive-listing broker should be obligated to do a reasonable amount of advertising and marketing in consideration of being given this special preference. A seller may further request guarantees of an all-out effort, with the right to terminate the listing if there is evidence of poor performance. Many brokers have second thoughts with this type of listing, which also gives the homeowner the right to sell. Some buyers will go directly to the seller and make a deal at a cheaper price, figuring they are eliminating commission costs for the seller. These buyers might very well have been generated from the brokerage firm's major advertising campaign. It does happen—and it happens often!

The exclusive-right-to-sell listing granted to the broker or firm that is a member of a multiple-listing organization is probably the most beneficial to both the real estate community and the homeowner. This method gives maximum exposure for the seller and complete protection to the brokers involved in an eventual sale.

Before making any firm or final commitments in the selection of the broker and type of listing arrangement, review your conclusions with your attorney and be guided by his or her advice. Do not sign any preprinted forms or contracts, even though they may state that such forms have been approved by a state or local bar association. Ask your attorney to explain in detail your obligations and the conditions under which you may terminate the listing agreement. Most real estate firms will request a listing period of a minimum of sixty days, usually much longer. If possible, limit the period to no longer than sixty days, but indicate a willingness to renew if you are satisfied with the performance. This gives you more flexibility and puts some pressure on the broker.

The right to function as a real estate broker is granted by a department within the state in which that broker operates. All states require that a broker pass a state examination to establish evidence of sufficient knowledge and education, good character, and integrity. The term *realtor* is a coined word which may only be used by an active member of a real estate board affiliated with the National Association of Real Estate Boards. A broker who is not a realtor is not necessarily more or less qualified than one who is. However, the designation realtor does signify high professional standards and ethics.

Over the past ten years, thousands of independently owned firms have become associated with nationally and internationally franchised real estate organizations. Those that have become affiliates must adhere to their organizations' rules, regulations, code of ethics, and standardized methods of operation. These franchises usually continue to be individually owned and operated, but they are clearly designated in all advertising and other public exposure as affiliates of the parent organization. At present, the largest in the United States is Century 21 Real Estate Corporation, with international headquarters in Irvine, California, boasting nearly 7,400 independently owned and operated franchises. Support services are administered through a network of thirty-three regions in the United States and Canada.

Among other national real estate franchising companies are Better Homes and Gardens, ERA, Gallery of Homes, Realty USA, Realty World, and Red Carpet. The primary advantage to the small- and medium-sized independent real estate office of being associated with a major referral network is the ability to compete effectively in the marketplace with larger firms. This coast-to-coast referral system provides marketing training, sales and managerial workshops, national and district advertising, and qualified professional brokers for relocation and investment purposes.

The seller of a home does have a distinct advantage in listing with a broker affiliated with a franchised broker, particularly in areas where there are large turnovers of executive personnel. Franchising offices do get a large percentage of referrals from other locales by brokers who are members of the same franchise. Keep in mind, though, that as most of these affiliated offices are independently owned and operated, the overall performance result to the homeowner will only be as good as the ability and efficiency of the owners and staff.

My personal observation regarding the value of a franchise-affiliated real estate office is that, with a few exceptions, it is a definite plus. The affiliation proves, in most cases, to have generated a special sense of pride, enthusiasm, and zest. Any spark that lights a fire under a sales organization is good.

And, as I say, the profession is becoming more and more specialized. Homeowners who think their property is worth a quarter of a million, half a million, a million, or more are turning to two unique international real estate firms whose forte it is to market luxury homes, farms, and estates. Their select clientele are among the richest and most powerful people in the world.

It is not my intention to compare their services or sing their praises, but simply to tell who they are, what they do, and how. If you are the proud owner of a luxury home or estate, I do, however, strongly recommend you seriously consider these two leading firms, whose reputation and credibility are impeccable.

They are (in alphabetical order to show no preference): Previews, Inc., 730 Fifth Avenue, New York, N.Y. 10019, and Sotheby Parke Bernet International Realty Corporation, 980 Madison Avenue, New York, N.Y. 10021. Both firms have regional offices in major cities throughout the United States and the world.

## Previews, Inc.

Since the early 1930s, Previews, Inc. has been responsible for the sale of everything from castles to cattle ranches and all that is unique and expensive in between. The firm is primarily interested in marketing the kinds of luxury homes and properties that demand a much broader exposure than the majority of local brokerage firms are able to offer. The organization is indeed selective and will not list the property for sale unless it is reasonably sure it meets the criteria of the firm's portfolio. If it does, the homeowner enters into an exclusive right-to-sell contract for three years, in those states which permit, with the provision that the property owner may cancel the listing by giving ninety days' notice.

Previews, Inc. requires as part of its contractual arrangement that the seller pay a maximum of 2 percent of the listing price in advance. This sum is expended for direct marketing costs, which are documented to the seller on request. They include, but are not limited to, the printing of extensive individual color brochures and the inclusion of the property in Previews, Inc.'s

*Homes International,* a quarterly publication which has a wide circulation and is distributed on most major airlines. Exposure of the property is also handled via other company publications, media advertising, direct mail, and video cassettes. The 2 percent maximum advance is adjusted downward on a sliding scale with multimillion-dollar properties.

The company has close contact with over 20,000 real estate brokers worldwide. It is through this vast network that the individual properties are shown and sold. However, if a seller specifically requests that only those directly employed by Previews, Inc. handle the property, the company will generally comply. The standard rate of commission charged is usually 11 percent of the final sale price, from which the 2 percent advance is subtracted at the time of closing. In the event the seller wishes to cancel during the agreement period, a portion of the advance fee is refunded.

While the firm's goal is to obtain Top Dollar for any client it represents, it will not accept a listing if extensive prelisting investigations reveal the property is overpriced. Trust the judgment of Previews, Inc.—the firm's brokers know what they're doing, and they do it well.

### Sotheby Parke Bernet International Realty Corporation

"For two hundred years we have been selling the best things off the walls. Now we're selling the best walls!"

Sotheby Parke Bernet has earned a worldwide reputation as one of the foremost firms in existence for collectors and sellers of fine art. While it continues to conduct renowned auctions for the art world, the recently founded international realty corporation subsidiary now provides a complete real estate brokerage service for selling luxury homes, estates, and farms.

One of the firm's primary marketing tools is its access to a large list of the most affluent people throughout the world. Its extensive resources include a worldwide office network, in-depth advertising experience, a computerized marketing program, and expert professional personnel.

The seller of a property is required to enter into a two-year exclusive right-to-sell agreement, in states which permit this, providing the property falls within the general guidelines of acceptable property for Sotheby Parke Bernet's high qualifications. The company requires the seller to advance, on an as-needed basis, a sum of money which normally comes to between 1 percent and 2 percent of the sale price. These funds are expended for direct marketing purposes, including promotional expense, advertising, mailings, and the preparation of thousands of elaborate brochures. The advance sums are not used for administrative costs, and a full accounting is supplied to the client. Generally, the commission rate is 10 percent of the sale price, and advance marketing expenses are fully credited against the sales commission at the time of closing. Most of the marketing of properties listed by the firm is done through a worldwide network of independent regional brokers on a cooperative commission basis. However, they do have fully licensed staffs at their principal offices who represent the company directly.

For those of you who feel your properties qualify for the services of either of these two very special firms and wish to explore further the possibility of listing with either, contact them by mail, phone, or in person. They will probably require substantial information before sending a representative to your home for a personal interview and evaluation. In the event a final listing agreement is not consummated, an inspection fee of varying costs might be charged, depending on individual circumstances.

*Whomever* you choose to sell your home accepts the tremendous responsibility and challenge of selling for Top Dollar. Selecting the real estate professional who will do this is *your* responsibility. Yet you may choose to sell your home by yourself, and some of you will be successful. Those of you who are not may find yourselves rereading this chapter. I hope it has made that job easier.

# 7

## *The Key to Trouble-Free Financing*

No one factor in the purchase of a home is more important than the availability of financing. It is a generally accepted legal procedure in most real estate contracts that purchase is contingent upon the buyer obtaining specified financing, usually in the form of a conventional mortgage loan. Financing is the key to whether the sale goes through or becomes the straw that breaks the camel's back.

If you have any doubt as to the truth of that statement, take heed of what happened to clients of mine earlier this year. An older couple, anxious to sell their home in Berkshire County, Massachusetts, and retire to Florida, had found a buyer who not only would pay close to their asking price but who had the down payment plus the income and the credit rating needed to obtain the mortgage. But that was just before their local savings institution was faced with dwindling money reserves (caused as more and more people were withdrawing their savings in favor of higher-interest-paying money-market funds) and was forced to reject nearly every other mortgage application submitted.

"I feel terrible about this," the mortgage officer told me, as he rejected my client's buyer, too. So did we, especially the owners who, in part, felt guilty, having withdrawn nearly $40,000 themselves only six months earlier. And now what they had been reading about in the newspaper had struck home—their home and their sale. However, I suggested a meeting be held at the bank. At that meeting the owners told the mortgage officer they would return the $40,000 *and* deposit at least another $60,000 of the purchase price in a three-year savings certificate, and the banker in turn approved the buyer's application for mortgage.

In normal times and under normal conditions, obtaining financing is a rather routine procedure. The strange thing is, whenever *you* wish to sell *your* home, nothing is normal. Any of the following could happen:

• Your buyer loses his job one week before closing and the bank withdraws its commitment.
• Your buyer's application is denied because the IRS filed a lien for back taxes.
• The bank appraiser thinks your home is not worth the asking price.
• The amount needed by the buyer exceeds the local lending institution's maximum limit available to any one borrower.

Other typical reasons for financing being refused include: insufficient down payment; too high ratio of debt to funds available; poor credit history; the buyer is unable to sell his present home; substantial increases in down-payment requirements or interest rates during the period between application and commitment. State usury laws contribute further to a mortgage pinch, and especially hard hit are those seeking to purchase a recreation, second, or country home.

If you have bought and sold more than one home during your lifetime, you are well aware of the problems involved in financing. First-time sellers should read this chapter carefully to achieve Top Dollar results with a miminum amount of aggravation and disappointment. There is a direct relationship between the sale of a home at the best price possible and the amount of liberal, long-term financing available. This is especially true under our present income tax laws, general economic conditions, and periods of runaway inflation.

During inflationary periods, money managers advise home buyers to borrow the maximum amount for the longest period possible (twenty-five to thirty years) at a fixed rate of interest. This widespread, generally accepted theory is based on the principle that as the homeowner's income and the value of his home increase with inflation, the mortgage payment remains the same, and the borrower makes these payments with cheaper and cheaper dollars. Present income tax laws—permitting full deduction of all interest charges relating to home ownership—add more credibility to this theory. The future homeowner is further advised to invest a minimum down payment from his own funds, and to place additional available funds in other investments, such as tax-free securities, art, gold, and other collectibles. Home ownership under this investment program provides one of the best "tax shelters" available to the individual. Indeed, it has become one of the contributing factors to the housing boom over the past several years.

Those individuals who are in high income tax brackets and are paying maximum rates for inadequate rented space do not receive any tax benefits from their rent receipts. Nor do they have a hedge against inflation. It has become a legend today that only fools have a burning-of-the-mortgage ceremony. The financial wizards will mortgage to the hilt and take the proceeds of their refinancing to buy another home or a bar of gold, or to send all the kids to college. Our great-grandfathers would probably shake their heads in amazement, but that's the way it is—1980's style. It is considered almost un-American to pay cash for anything.

The jury is still out considering this philosophy, and the verdict will be in when this economic cycle either changes or continues to escalate. But one thing is certain in this period of unprecedented inflation and high income taxes—if you want to sell your home, it is a must that financing be available to the buyer! Where it comes from is another question.

Over one-third of the states in the country have antiquated usury laws limiting the amount of interest banking institutions or lenders may charge a would-be borrower. Savings and loans and other thrift institutions, the primary sources for home mortgages, are further limited legally as to the amount of interest they can offer their depositors. Those with savings accounts chase the highest rate, which has recently been available in various money markets, tax-free bonds, and other securities, draining to record lows the amounts available to savings organizations for home-mortgage financing. When interest rates soar, commercial banks find it much more lucrative to make short-term business loans, which are not covered by usury laws, thus contributing to the mortgage crunch. In states where usury laws are now nonexistent or usury limits are more in line with the going interest rates, more homes are selling.

The consensus of opinion throughout the banking community is that we are rapidly approaching the demise of the typical conventional mortgage as we have known it since the early 1930s. The fixed rate of interest for twenty- to twenty-five-year periods, with the same monthly payment of principal and interest, either has been or will be replaced by a mortgage loan of less than twenty years, with a variable interest rate. The rate, based on the prevailing prime interest rate, or on a similar basis, would fluctuate up or down with the standard used. Another concept for mortgage loans is to extend the mortgage under the conventional loan principal for twenty to twenty-five years, but to make it callable (with the full amount of balance due or renewed at the option of the lender) every five years. These rather extreme changes in the conventional mortgage market result in part from the complex fluctuations in the Federal Reserve system regulating the banking industry and the chaos in international money markets.

It is interesting to note most homeowners' attitudes and stubborn, head-in-the-sand reactions to prevailing mortgage problems when they are ready to sell. They listen half-heartedly, casually regarding the erosion of mortgage financing—which may turn the Great American Dream of home ownership into a nightmare—as the "buyer's problem." They believe their homes will be easily sold to people who will pay all cash—people such as an Arab prince or an executive or a professional with a lot of clout at the local bank. But for those who are conservative, realistic, and a bit pessimistic, I offer the following guidelines to financing the sale of your home in good times or bad.

If you wish to sell for Top Dollar, be prepared to become involved. Do not think for a moment that you can walk away and "leave it to beaver," even though all the beavers are eager and experienced. Remember, *financing is the key to your sale.*

Most chapters in this book emphasize owner involvement and awareness. Prior to any successful sale, you must first determine your personal and financial priorities and find out what chunk, if any, will be removed by income taxes. Your tax status may be so critical that you must become involved in taking back a mortgage rather than accepting all cash and getting clobbered with a huge income tax liability. On the other hand, if you expect to build or purchase another home, condominium, or co-op with all or part of the proceeds from the sale of your home, the opportunity to finance a would-be buyer simply would not conform to your plans.

In an attempt to simplify what appears to be a complex analysis, put the horse before the cart and ask yourself or your advisers the following questions:

• Do I want an all-cash transaction?
• What will I have left after taxes?

- Do I need the proceeds from the sale to live on or to buy another home?
- Should I postpone selling if, because of negative local or national economic conditions, my only option is to become involved in financing?

With clear answer to these questions prior to the formal listing of your home, you will be prepared to establish the perimeters within which all those involved can intelligently function in your best interests. The more flexibility in financing a purchaser has available, the easier it is to put the deal together.

Consult with the officers of a lending institution who know you and your property well. The bank that held or is presently holding your mortgage should be your first port of call. Determine from the bank's officers their present mortgage policy and a reasonable guesstimate of the maximum amount of mortgage available to a credit-worthy applicant. They may either respond without hesitation or be reluctant to give you any specifics unless you file a formal application for mortgage or remortgage, paying the required appraisal and inspection fee (usually under $100). If a fee is required, it is worth the investment as this procedure has a two-pronged benefit. It will help in establishing the asking price and will also lay the foundation for a purchaser's borrowing needs.

Lending policies usually conform to a pattern of offering a percentage of the bank's market-value appraisal of the property. For example: Your bank will lend 70 percent of the appraised value, and you are planning to list the property at $100,000; therefore, the mortgage available would be $70,000. If the bank only offers $60,000 after inspection, view this as a red flag— you have either overpriced your property, in the bank's opinion, or that bank might have a maximum limit it will extend on any one home, regardless of market value. It is imperative that you be familiar with this information *before* your purchaser applies for a mortgage—and not *after!*

If a purchaser agrees to pay an amount near your asking price, files an application for a mortgage, and is refused because the bank's appraisal of the property amounts to less than the purchaser is willing to pay, his first reaction is that he has been taken. The normal course of action for the purchaser is then to restructure the offer in accordance with the bank's appraisal or to withdraw it entirely. Therefore, it is in your best interest not to be placed in this uncomfortable and vulnerable position of having to compromise or start the selling process all over again with a new buyer. (Where there are several lending institutions in a community, mortgage and appraisal policies will vary. A definite problem exists in areas served by only one or two prime lending sources. Check with all other available lending institutions serving your area if the results obtained from *your* bank are disappointing.)

Once you have determined the availability of mortgage financing from all possible sources—including FHA (Federal Housing Administration) insured loans, VA guaranteed loans (GI loans), Farmer's Home Administration (Federal Land Bank), and private mortgage brokerage firms—you are in an enviable position, if your credit-worthy purchaser is able to qualify.

If the amount of mortgage financing is limited by the lender's internal policy or federal and state regulations, investigate whether any of those lenders are associated with a privately insured lending program, such as Mortgage Guarantee Insurance Corporation (MGIC) of Milwaukee, Wisconsin. If so, this rather new concept in home financing will enable the home purchaser to obtain a conventional mortgage of up to 95 percent of the appraised property value at the prevailing rate of interest. The borrower will pay a one-time insurance charge and a monthly fee representing a premium to be paid to the insurance company. This program guarantees to the lending institution that portion of the mortgage loan that is in excess of its limitation (usually 70 or 80 percent of appraised value). MGIC does not lend the money; it only insures the excess risk for the bank over conventional limits. This attractive opportunity enables a purchaser to obtain a $100,000 home with only a $5,000 cash down payment. The amounts of both the one-time charge and the monthly fee vary with the amount of the mortgage.

When liberal or normal mortgage financing is not available, you *must* consider as one alternative becoming involved in financing all or part of your buyer's requirements in order to sell your home. This is especially true with the tightening of the money market. Here are some actual case histories showing that the key to the sale was the seller's willingness to participate in the financing:

🔺 The buyer agreed to purchase a home for $80,000 but didn't have the 30 percent ($24,000) down payment required to meet the best mortgage financing available. All he did have was $15,000; therefore, $9,000 was lacking. The bank had agreed to extend a mortgage loan in the amount of $56,000 (70 percent of $80,000). So where did the $9,000 come from? The seller. The purchaser gave the seller a second mortgage as security for the $9,000, to be paid in monthly installments over a period of five years at 10 percent interest. At closing, the seller received $71,000 in cash ($15,000 from the buyer and $56,000 from the bank) and the second mortgage receivable for $9,000.

🔺 The seller and buyer agreed to a $140,000 selling price for a home. The buyer did not require any mortgage financing but was unable to close the transaction until his present home, located in another state and on the market for $200,000, was sold. Confirmation of the value of the buyer's present home was made available by his selling broker and banker (full credit report on the purchaser and letters of recommendation of credit were also given to the seller). The buyer offered the seller $50,000 in cash and asked him to take back a mortgage (purchase-money mortgage) as collateral, in addition to a personal note for $90,000, for a maximum of two years. The buyer further requested that no principal payments be required, but said he would pay interest on the $90,000 monthly at 12 percent. The buyer's home was sold eighteen months after the closing, and the mortgage was paid in full.

● A credit-worthy purchaser was unable to obtain $60,000 in mortgage financing from the available institution, which had a $40,000 ceiling limit for any one individual. The seller needed all funds from his home in order to purchase a retirement home in another community and thus could not offer mortgage financing himself. Therefore, the real estate broker involved in the transaction made arrangements with a local commercial bank for a personal loan for the buyer in the amount of $20,000 needed. The bank required a guarantee for half the $20,000. The seller agreed to cosign up to $10,000 of the $20,000 note. The buyer agreed to give a second mortgage in the amount of $10,000 as security if, for any reason, he defaulted in paying the full $20,000 bank loan. The buyer made all payments promptly and liquidated the $20,000 obligation within three years.

● A young, recently married couple, anxious to purchase a home for $52,000 from a Top Dollar seller, did not qualify for mortgage, as they lacked credit history and permanent employment status, and had only a $5,000 cash down payment. They did have good character references and specialized training, and were both currently employed. Local bank officials informed the seller that the couple would be likely candidates for mortgage once an additional $5,000 had been saved and their present employment positions had advanced. The owner agreed to take back mortgage in the amount of $47,000 on the basis of a twenty-five-year amortization payment, thus making monthly payments comfortable for the couple. The mortgage further provided that the entire principal payments remaining had to be paid in full three years from the date of the closing; this is known as a "balloon" payment. The buyers applied for and received bank financing for the amount due two and a half years after closing and paid the mortgage in full.

● The buyer received a commitment from a lending institution for all the financing needed to acquire the seller's home for $137,500. Because of an unexpected emergency three weeks before closing, he was short $7,000 toward the down payment. Bank policy did not permit second-mortgage financing for home acquisition. The seller became skeptical and demanded solid protection and collateral for the $7,000. The attorney for the seller recommended that the client proceed with the transaction, providing the buyer would give a chattel mortgage (lien) on equipment owned by him and used in his business. The buyer agreed and reduced the $7,000 obligation in one year to $3,200.

● The seller listed his home for $195,000 (purchased six years ago for $85,000). The highest offer received in six months was $160,000. A buyer agreed to pay $187,500, but would not pay the 17 percent prevailing interest rate, plus four points for a $100,000 approved mortgage from a local banking institution. He requested that the seller take back a purchase-money mortgage for $100,000 for twenty years at 14 percent. He also agreed to raise his offer from $187,500 to $190,000 if the seller would agree to the mortgage terms requested. Because there was top-notch credit information available about this high-income purchaser, the seller agreed. Mortgage payments were timely met for one year, at which time the buyer resold the house for $225,000 and the mortgage was paid in full.

● The owner of a Florida condominium had obtained a $50,000 mortgage at 8 percent at the time it was purchased for $70,000. The buyer was willing to pay the asking price of $92,500 (comparable condominiums in the same building were selling for only $85,000) providing the seller would agree to let him pay only the mortgage payments and any maintenance costs (*i.e.* no down payment) for three years. Then he would make full payment in one lump sum, less, of course, the amount paid toward the mortgage principal during that time period. The seller agreed, and a contract embodying these terms was executed. When this contract was signed, the buyer took possession but leased the apartment to another person for the three years. At the end of that time, he retired, sold his home in the northeast, paid off the seller, and moved into the apartment himself.

♠ A contract for the sale of a home was executed at the sale price of $125,000, contingent upon the buyer assuming the seller's present mortgage in the amount of $65,800. The lending institution approved the application of the buyer for the mortgage balance, but notified the seller (original borrower) that the commitment was made to the purchaser on a "subject-to-the-mortgage purchase, rather than an assumption basis." This meant that if the buyer defaulted on the mortgage, the seller would be personally obligated in the event of foreclosure for the negative difference between what the property brought and the mortgage balance. The commitment further demanded that the 10-1/2 percent present interest rate be increased to 15 percent. This could place the seller in a precarious position in the event that property values declined or that the buyer did not meet payments on time. The matter was resolved by the bank's agreeing to release the obligation of the seller in full, executing a satisfaction of mortgage to the seller after three years from the date of closing, if, until that time, all payments by the buyer were timely met. It should be noted that the purchaser was unable to obtain any other mortgage financing in the area, even though his credit history was good.

♠ A co-op apartment buyer offered $280,000 for an apartment listed at $310,000. The policy of the co-op building directors did not permit any financing in excess of 50 percent of sale price ($140,000). The buyer was financially able to pay cash for purchase but did not wish to sell his tax-free income securities and wanted the maximum interest deduction for tax-shelter purposes. On the other hand, the seller had made a formal commitment to buy a home for $270,000 with proceeds from sale of his co-op and did not wish to obtain any financing for the purchase of his new home. The buyer obtained a $140,000 co-op loan, gave a note to the seller for $140,000 at 15 percent interest, and assigned to the seller $150,000 worth of market-value securities as collateral for the loan. The seller borrowed $140,000 from a commercial bank on the strength of the collateralized note, bought his new home, and did not have to mortgage it.

♠ The seller of a home anticipated a taxable capital gain on his sale in the amount of $110,000. Because of age, he did not qualify for the $100,000 tax exemption available to sellers of principal residences. He was also unable to defer payment of tax under reinvestment provisions of the tax law, as he did not plan to purchase another home. He was able to get Top Dollar for luxury home from a buyer requesting 80 percent financing. The seller decided to accept the offer and take advantage of the installment-sale reporting method for income tax purposes by taking 30 percent or less of a down payment in the year of sale, thus saving over $10,000 in taxes, as opposed to taking all cash or taking more than 30 percent down payment in the year of sale.

Now, more important, let's look at what you can do to structure a sale—and still get Top Dollar for your home, co-op, or condominium—during the bad times when:

- *No* mortgage money is available from the usual prime banks and mortgage-lending institutions.
- The amount an individual mortgage may be is limited to $40,000 or less, and then at high double-digit interest rates.
- Banks and other lending sources no longer permit a buyer to

assume the seller's present mortgage, unless the applicant is willing to accept a substantial increase in the existing interest rate being charged for that mortgage.

- Would-be borrowers are asked by a lender to pay an origination fee, or "points," a one-time service charge of a few hundred to several thousand dollars depending upon the amount of mortgage approved.

- Limited mortgage financing is available only to those who can come up with a substantial down payment (in excess of 30 percent) on the property being purchased.

- Some mortgages, in states where laws permit, are granted only if the lender has the right to increase the interest rate every few years (this increase, again if substantial, could put the buyer in a precarious financial position later on).

- The lid on maximum interest rate allowable by law (usury law) has been lifted by federal or state legislation or special directive.

- Other types of loans, whether secured or not, are difficult, if not impossible, to obtain from commercial banks or lending institutions. Or, if available, they are granted only on a short-term basis at record-breaking interest rates.

- Great numbers of ready-to-sign buyers are being rejected by mortgage lenders because they cannot prove, as a prerequisite to filing a mortgage application, that they make well above the national salary average and have been employed for some time.

- Some mortgage commitments are being issued but contain clauses such as "at prevailing interest rates at day of closing," "subject to funds available," or "providing no negative major financial changes occur in applicant's net worth statement or income from date of application to closing."

When any or all of these situations exist, there's a good chance that your potential buyer will be faced with a road block, unless, of course, the overall financial mess takes a turn for the better—and it could!

In the meantime, however, you and your real estate representative(s) will need to work out a financial solution for the buyer. And, take my word for it, it's being done every day. True, the solution may not always be simple or orthodox, but if it works for you—and your buyer—then do it!

What's more, despite whatever happens, keep in mind that savings and loan associations, or other thrift-type institutions that loan mortgage funds to millions of home buyers each year, remain, for the most part, in a healthy financial position. In fact, even during tough times, they might well be compared to the good, stable American family: They're generating an above-average income, and their assets exceed their liabilities—they're only a little short of cash! Thus, remember that when attempting to structure a sale during bad times, the cash you stand to receive, if your home is sold, can be used as clout with the bank. So don't hesitate to use it as needed leverage so that your prospective buyer can obtain a mortgage.

For instance, if you presently have a hefty mortgage at a low interest rate, tell your bank or lending institution you will deposit $20,000 or $30,000 from the proceeds of your sale in a lower paying interest account for 3 or 4 years, providing it permits your credit-worthy buyer to assume your present mortgage at only 2 or 3 percentage points above your existing rate. After all, if they don't do that, tell them they may be stuck with that lower rate for another 15 years if you don't sell the house! Chances are, however, you won't need to say anything because many banks will view the deposit you offer as a nice sum of money they can lend out at a good profit. And besides, this plan does indeed give the bank a higher interest rate than it is earning on your present mortgage. Then again, if the bank is reluctant to live with this "new" mortgage rate, it may agree to do so if your buyer will agree to accept a higher rate at the end of say, 5 years. And he or she probably will.

Now, let us assume your buyer is willing to pay the interest rate requested for a new mortgage, but is short $10,000 of the $30,000 down payment required by the lending institution extending that mortgage. In this case, tell the bank you will deposit $16,000 of the $20,000 he can put down in a savings account at an interest rate lower than the highest paid until such time as your buyer can make a substantial number of payments on the mortgage—three years would be a fair limit.

You have sweetened the cash position of the lending institution by $6,000 more than it would have if your buyer came up with the full down payment. "But, why should I leave $16,000 in that bank at a lower interest rate than I can get from a money-market fund?" you may ask. Well, you can't have your cake and eat it too! If you want to get Top Dollar for your home, you may have to sacrifice a few hundred dollars a year in interest, which, in addition, will probably be taxed fully, as opposed to a more favorable capital gain tax advantage you might receive by using those proceeds differently. Besides, the rest of the profit obtained from selling your home at Top Dollar can always be placed in higher-interest money markets, thus drawing *some* additional income for you, which won't happen if you're still sitting there waiting for a buyer to get a mortgage!

And yet, for those of you who have no mortgage, or live in an area where mortgage funds are either non-existent or extremely limited, you must be receptive to taking back a good-size mortgage from a credit-worthy buyer willing to pay Top Dollar, at an interest rate that will turn that buyer on. Then too, structure a mortgage that might make the deal even more attractive to your buyer: Offer an interest-only mortgage for the first year or two, and let the buyer amortize that mortgage over 35 years (this will keep the monthly payment low), *but* add the provision that the entire principal sum remaining is due in full at the end of 5 or 10 years. At this time, the "callable period," your buyer will probably be in a position to refinance through a banking institution and pay you off.

Some of you, I realize, will need the net proceeds from the sale of your home in order to purchase another home and thus are not in a position to offer any mortgage financing. You, too, might think about purchasing your next home from a seller who will structure *your* deal the same way. Or, you might consider renting a home for the few years until your buyer's "callable" amount becomes due, when you will receive your proceeds in full.

Remember, too, it is not uncommon, especially during bad times, to let a buyer rent or lease your home at well above the normal fee, that is, until the mortgage market improves. This is especially true when you must leave that home, if not the community. And yet, a word of caution: This could mean the loss of thousands of dollars! By that I mean, if you rent your house for an extended period it might be considered by the IRS as a business or rental property and not a principal residence, thus eliminating those liberal tax advantages that apply only to principal residence. Be sure to discuss this matter with your attorney or tax adviser.

On the other hand, hardly a day goes by without some would-be seller telling someone in my office that because they fear a drop in prices, a major recession, and massive unemployment, they will not take back a mortgage. They figure they do not want to be in a position of having to foreclose if their buyer defaults —and having to resell their home in a deflated market at that. This is not at all an uncommon reaction, particularly from those who remember vividly the era of the Great Depression. Now, if you share this feeling and fear that taking back a first or second mortgage is not all that secure a move, then ask your buyer to give you additional collateral in the form of a life insurance policy or assignment of a pension account, negotiable securities, or various other collectibles, in addition to the mortgage. It is not unreasonable to ask the buyer for an assignment of any income disability policy, in the event of illness, as well. But also state that these extra guarantees will be released when at least half of the mortgage amount due you has been paid. In other words, if you feel more secure wearing both a belt *and* suspenders, then by all means do so!

These are but a few of several solutions I've personally used to help clients sell their homes throughout the years, whether in good times or bad. When it comes to *structuring* your sale, I hope this will show you that such solutions do exist—and work —and that all it takes is a little imagination and effort to get yourself seated at the closing table.

# 8

## *The Tricky Question: Which Offer Is Best for You?*

Regardless of how much the final offer differs from your asking price, do not delay in making some reasonable counterproposal as a matter of courtesy and to keep the ball bouncing. Consideration might be given to including the stained glass dining room fixture in your counterproposal. Though its present market value might only be $1,500, the prospective buyer will appraise it higher to justify agreeing to your position. This volley of offer-and-counteroffer can begin early, with the firm commitment of the buyer well in place, and it is up to you not to lose this advantage by having him withdraw because of your inability to keep the volley going or because you dropped the ball. Nothing is gained by having the prospective buyer informed directly or otherwise by your agents that you are considering additional offers, taking the home off the market for the time being, or any other cheap-shot pressure tactics (even if true) that are too often used.

And yet, in some cases, your evaluation of one or more offers will be based on matters less tangible than money alone. For instance, I can recall one couple who lived in the Catskill Mountains and who, only a short while after placing their home of some thirty years on the market, had not one but two good offers to consider. The first was made by a couple from the city who, although they turned their nose up at the owner's idea of interior decoration, offered just $1,000 less than the asking price.

The other offer, however, came from a young couple, recently transferred to the area from the midwest, who not only *loved* everything about the house but who, in many ways, reminded the owners of themselves so many years ago when they had bought the home. In fact, the young wife already had one child and was pregnant with another, as was the owner's wife when they moved in. Well, needless to say, the present owners accepted the young couple's offer, even though it was a couple of thousand below their asking price—and they helped with the financing to boot.

If you expect to sell your home, you should also expect to negotiate with one or more prospective buyers, even though your asking price has been based on the best professional advice available. For naturally it is rare for a buyer to pay that price. That only happens in Utopia. And I can tell you, in more than thirty years of selling homes, I have only been to Utopia a couple of times, and I can attest that it's an unreal world.

Once, for instance, there were three elderly bachelors who had been operating a small dairy farm of about 120 acres in upstate New York all of their lives. But now they wanted to sell the place for $135,000. And, within only ten days after listing it, a man came into the office and offered to buy it at the asking price. "Why, I never thought the Tompkin brothers would sell the place," their next-door neighbor remarked. "And I've been wanting to set my eldest son up on a spread of his own...but not too far away."

It was as simple as that. Whereas we were looking to dicker with some folks from the city who may have liked the old stone house but had no use for the barns and all the land, the buyer was actually in our own backyard—literally.

But, as I say, this doesn't happen very often, and, when it does, the result is not the elation you would expect. Instead, everyone begins to wonder, "What did I do wrong? Could I have gotten more money?" You can't win, so perhaps it is better that, in most cases anyway, there is the dickering and haggling one would expect in horse trading.

In many cases timing is the most important factor when it comes to evaluating offers. Rarely are the first few offers accepted, even though they may only be five or ten thousand dollars below the asking price. This is especially true if they come fast and furiously within only a short time after the property has been on the market. However, there is more truth than fiction to the old cliché, "the first offer is usually the best.".

The first reaction, though, by a seller to any offer less than the asking price is one of rebellion, frustration, and ill feeling toward both the real estate agent and the prospective buyer. The buyer's response to his rejected offer is disappointment and a bit of antagonism. The role of the agent-as-referee is to be calm, cool, and collected, and to employ professional gentleness.

The considerations in evaluating offers are varied and many. Naturally, a seller who is under pressure because of financial, personal, or similar reasons has to be more flexible than one who can afford to wait for a better offer. These two categories—"forced sellers" and "willing sellers"—often represent the difference between just selling at a good price or getting Top Dollar. Time and motivation head the list of factors to consider in evaluating any and all offers. Others are: personal status; national and local economic conditions; price range of the property; availability of liberal mortgage financing; real or potential environmental problems; and quality, size and condition of the home. Although these considerations should have been taken into account when establishing the asking price, there is often a tendency by the seller to subconsciously ignore them when considering offers.

Time is not always a luxury for the seller; in fact, hard evidence has shown that in cases where time was of the essence, values have been reduced to 50 percent or the property has been made totally unmarketable by waiting. National examples include homes within a reasonable distance of the Three Mile Island Nuclear Power Plant in Pennsylvania, the Love Canal area near Buffalo, New York, and coastal areas battered by hurricanes in the summer of 1979. These abnormal, unpredictable, and isolated events do happen in this ever-changing world, along with massive forest fires, droughts and floods—and they have serious repercussions in the real estate market.

On the other hand, values have tripled in less than one year in places—Palm Springs; Los Angeles; San Francisco; Boca Raton; Houston; Stamford, Connecticut; Hilton Head, North Carolina; and co-op apartments in New York City. Luck, either good or bad, and a blend of genius and judgment either adds to or subtracts from acceptance or rejection of an offer.

An additional ingredient is an evaluation of the credibility of potential buyers. Seasoned real estate people can usually separate "conversation" from reality, as one of their primary functions is to qualify a buyer and obtain a formal, firm commitment prior to presenting an offer to the seller. What does all this mean? Simply, the real estate agent should determine that the prospective buyer is capable of backing up the offer financially, legally, and morally. Some over-zealous and naive real estate representatives will approach a seller prior to having this firm commitment from an interested buyer. The seller might accept the proposal and agree to lowering the price of the home, only to find out a few hours later that the prospective buyer had a change of heart. Under no circumstances should you respond to any offers without being assured that they are in writing and are accompanied by evidence of good faith. Otherwise, you may be evaluating a fishing expedition rather than an offer.

In addition to the offering price, a proposal should include the date the buyer wishes to close and occupy, the amount and source of financing needed, personal property to be included, and the name of the buyer's attorney or law firm. Other contingencies to be specified in a proposal include house inspection, surveys, title insurance, and anything else expected to be part of a formal contract. This is also the time to learn whether the buyer must sell a present home before proceeding with negotiations. This type of commitment in time and effort will separate the doer from the dreamer.

Placing your home on the market with the attitude that you will *not* waver from the asking price, will *not* consider including some personal property—such as stoves and refrigerators—will *not* share in some of the various closing costs normally paid for by the purchaser, will *not* participate in any owner financing whatsoever, in short, will not be flexible in any way, is definitely a credit to your strong character. It will also be a small miracle if you ever get to a closing.

Let us assume your home is on the market for $125,000 and you receive a solid offer in the amount of $115,000, or $10,000 less than Top Dollar. Further assume that you do not have to participate in the financing and the buyer is in a position to close the transaction within thirty days. Your first reaction to this offer will probably be negative, particularly if it is presented to you within a short time after listing.

Now, although you do not have any urgent need to sell at this time and are willing to wait six months to get your price, consider what it will cost you directly or indirectly to maintain your residence for the next half year.

To determine the net economic gain or loss from rejecting the offer at hand, a reasonable computation of the six months' costs is as follows:

| | |
|---|---:|
| Interest income lost | |
| (approximately 10 percent x $125,000) | $6,000 |
| Property taxes | 1,500 |
| Utilities | 600 |
| Insurance | 300 |
| Miscellaneous | 600 |
| Total | *$9,000 |

In the event that, six months from the date of your present $115,000 offer, you did receive your asking price of $125,000, the net difference between the two offers ($1,000) would be nil.

The above computation, which reflects the loss of interest from the money you could have placed in the bank at 10 percent interest or more, is generally overlooked by most sellers when giving consideration to the cost of living in their home. As in the example cited, for those of you who do not have a mortgage balance, the loss of interest item is substantial. The carrying costs for those who do have a mortgage balance will probably net the same conclusion, as mortgage payments would have to be made during the given period.

Serious buyers who make firm commitments usually leave room for future negotiations. Getting a handle on how far they will go before making a U-turn involves more than dollars and sense. It is important to establish a firm but warm relationship with your hopeful successor in an effort to determine his emotional involvement, obvious alternatives, family influence, past and present life-styles, and general character. It is equally important to impress prospective purchasers that you truly care

---

*This amount does not, however, reflect what it would cost you to live elsewhere during that same period.

about them. Touching base over a cup of coffee with the people who have made an offer and leading the discussion to everything except the price of the home reduces tensions and gives you the opportunity to make a graceful counterproposal.

An overly chummy buyer-seller relationship prior to a firm commitment by both parties is not advised. But nor do I share the opinion of many in the real estate profession that purchaser and seller should be kept miles apart until the day of closing. There should be a happy medium with one exception: Discussion of details relating to the purchase price and other hard-line facets of the transaction should be left *entirely* to the real estate representative and/or attorneys.

# 9

## *Does It Go with the House?*

A real estate transaction will bring out the best in human nature—and the worst! Everything the seller has is worth a fortune, but not to the buyer—until the seller makes it known it is *not* included in the sale. Sellers have been known to remove every light bulb in the house, including the one in the refrigerator, the night before the closing. One-hundred-thousand-dollar transactions have blown up at the closing table over a piece of worn-out carpeting on a stairwell or a motorless washing machine removed at the last moment.

It has been my experience that personal property *should not* be part of the offering. To avoid normal hassles accompanying negotiations for the sale of property, the seller should decide well in advance of listing the property what specific items he wishes to remove or keep. Lighting fixtures, chandeliers, fireplace equipment, special built-ins, stoves and refrigerators, fine hardware and ornaments are generally assumed to be part of the deal once the home has been shown with these items in place. Drapes, shades, television antennas, lawn and garden equipment, and supplies for swimming pools and tennis courts are a few more examples of why attorneys, realtors, buyers, and sellers scream at each other along the way.

The average seller from Albany to Albuquerque has a philosophy of personal property that is: "If I get my price, sure, I'll leave them all!" But in the real world two things normally happen: They don't get their price; and Aunt Susie wants to reclaim the fireplace screen she gave them for a wedding present. And then the fur begins to fly, and so does the buyer— right out the front door!

It is not always possible or practical to physically remove during the early showing periods of the transaction all the items not included in the sale. If this is the case, all prospective buyers should be definitely informed and given specific lists of items *not* included in the asking price. The owner or owner's representative should avoid any discussion regarding personal property until such time as the contract for the real property has been executed. (Most state laws define real property as that which is permanently affixed to the land and all that which is permanently affixed to the building. Therefore, I hope you will not think about removing your favorite toilet bowl or doorknob on the morning of the closing—believe me, this has been done before —under the assumption that these items are personal property.)

This is the question: Will your home sell any faster and for more money if you include many of these personal property goodies? Perhaps not. The majority of buyers feel they have overpaid until ten minutes after closing, when they assure themselves they have made the best buy in the world. Therefore, they will take for granted and not appreciate the best intentions of the seller. Certainly, there are exceptions. But they only apply to your neighbors who recently sold *their* home. The primary objective of the seller is to sell the real property. This is *not* the moment to be a one-time furniture, antique, or garden-equipment dealer. The buyer of your home should be given the first option to purchase the contents and miscellaneous items you wish to sell *after* the closing, not *before!*

There are buyers who will present offers on a lock, stock, and barrel basis. They are sincere, and a seller must consider their presentation seriously, as this may be the best way to obtain Top Dollar with the least amount of aggravation and delay. Usually, this type of offer is made not necessarily by those who are looking for a bargain but by those who don't have the time or patience to furnish and equip the home. The primary pitfall is that once this type of arrangement has been mutually agreed upon, the seller begins the nit-picking process of removing or replacing the hand-made crocheted bedspread with a Sears Roebuck reproduction, the brass doorknocker with the two screws that held it in place, and the Irish linen handtowels with a collection of Handiwipes. What happens the day of the closing? No closing.

Reading this, your immediate reaction is: "Well, I wouldn't do anything like that!" If you agree to sell everything, it will mean *everything*—including your dishes, linens, silverware, ashtrays, vases, bric-a-brac, right down to your favorite portable TV in the den. There are many all-or-nothing deals and one should be prepared both psychologically and realistically for the possibility of having to handle them. Our files are jammed with contracts and memos of good intentions. But somewhere along the way, something happened, usually petty or stubborn, and the file was marked DTD (down the drain!). Many people involved in a real estate transaction think they are dealing solely with bricks and mortar. But the success or failure rests with the best and worst qualities of human nature.

I do not generally agree with the consensus of opinion that showing a home furnished and equipped is a positive selling factor in contrast to showing no furnishings at all. It is a rare buyer who does not secretly criticize the type of furnishings another has or the untidiness or sterility of setting, or quietly envy the antiques and art he or she cannot afford. Attention is normally focused on the contents, thereby diverting the purpose of the sale, which is the home itself, and leaving the buyer either too frustrated or too depressed to make an offer. This would not happen if the props were removed. The four walls of any home can stand by themselves. But the taste of the seller within those four walls rarely matches the taste of the buyer.

If you plan to occupy your home while it is on the market, then include the following in the asking price as basic "go-with-the-home" personal property items: curtains and drapery rods, television antennas, wall-to-wall carpeting, venetian blinds, fireplace screen and grate, stove and refrigerator, and a few lawn and garden tools. Unusual mailboxes, bird baths, markers, and weathervanes should certainly be left with the property. The sellers of most above-average-size homes and estates might consider leaving one riding lawn mower or tractor.

In summary:

- Don't get involved in the sale of any of your personal property to the buyer at least until the contract for sale of the home has been executed.
- If specific fixtures or attached items are definitely not being sold with the home, either remove them prior to showing or make definitive representations to all concerned that they are not included in the sale.
- If a buyer is insistent on wanting one or two items of personal property, don't make a mountain out of a molehill if this smooths the way to a successful closing.
- Don't lose sight of your primary objective—which is selling your home for thousands of dollars—while vacillating over an old kitchen set worth just a few bucks.
- If you are getting Top Dollar, give more, not less, whether it is appreciated or not. You will feel good after the closing.

# 10

## *Why Does It Take So Long?*

The contract has been signed, the deposit check from the buyer has been received and safely put aside in your attorney's escrow account, the sun is shining, and the anxiety is over. Not quite. The engagement has been announced, but a hundred and one things can go wrong before the wedding.

Your first concern during this period is to expedite whatever has to be done to eliminate the contingencies that might rescind the agreement if not met or performed on time. Those things which are usually the worst trouble makers at this time are:

(1) Obtaining mortgage for the buyer;

(2) Receiving a green light from the title company;

(3) Passing the outside appraisal and engineering report with good marks;

(4) Getting the surveyor's stamp of approval that what you are selling is all there.

Your goal, and that of your realtor—who is just as anxious to have the sale go through as you are—is to eliminate these four major stumbling blocks. Your involvement in the contract-to-closing period is crucial. Much has to be done.

## Mortgage Approval

Contact the bank where the buyer has applied for a mortgage and deliver to the mortgage officer a photocopy of your deed, map, or survey of the property; explicit directions from the bank to your home (make a diagram); two good, recent small photos; and a brief, typed description, without flowery adjectives, of the home and other amenities. Try to determine the date of inspection by the bank, outside appraiser, or inspection committee. Advise your real estate representative that you wish to be at home the day of the bank inspection. Your presence is important at the time a mortgage inspection is made to answer the pertinent questions that might be asked.

Refrain from overselling or delaying the inspectors. *Do not* solicit from them any of their findings or question whether the mortgage will be approved. Their report to the bank is imperative, but the final decision for commitment or rejection rests with the institutional board or financing committee. It is worth pointing out various improvements that might be overlooked during the normal inspection, but do not bore the inspectors with details and items they have seen a thousand times. The inspection process is not as mechanical as one might think, and it is for this reason that a pleasant, comfortable, honest, and positive seller will make a better impression than one who leaves a note saying, "Be back in an hour."

It is not advisable for you to call the lending institution after the inspection to inquire as to mortgage status. When a decision has been reached, your attorney and/or realtor will be promptly notified. It usually takes thirty to forty-five days for a mortgage application to be processed and acted upon. (Buyers have a tendency to delay completing the mortgage application forms.) Keeping open the lines of communication between seller, buyer, and realtor will expedite the process of obtaining credit and employment information required from the buyer and hasten the decision from the lending institution.

### Contract Status

Once all of the terms to be embodied in the contract of sale have been resolved by the buyer, the seller, and their respective attorneys, the document itself is usually signed first by the buyer or buyers. It is at this time that the buyer submits the agreed deposit, usually in the amount of 10 percent of the selling price. These funds are normally held by the attorney for the seller in a special escrow account until closing. If the contract is legally voided, they are returned to the buyer. It is not unreasonable for the buyer to ask that the attorney place the deposit funds in an interest-bearing account during the contract period. The interest earned is worthy of consideration, particularly in transactions involving substantial deposits. Here again is another grey area for buyer/seller tensions. Frequently, sellers believe the interest earned is theirs, while buyers insist it belongs to them. I would not recommend making an issue out of this. It is not worth risking the delay or a possible "blowup" of the entire deal over what is usually less than a few hundred dollars. Either offer to split the interest or forget it. Be thankful the buyer is signing and putting up a substantial deposit, and keep your perspective.

There is a logistical problem when buyers and sellers and their respective attorneys do not reside locally. Prolonging the signing of contracts because of mailing delays might extend the closing period or result in a complete change of heart by the buyer. Request frequent progress reports from your attorney or realtor about the contract-signing status, particularly as to handling and mailing. The fully executed contract is often requested by lending institutions as part of a mortgage application. Any delay in producing this document will delay the mortgage process.

A seller is not able to make any firm commitments regarding future plans until the contract of sale has been fully signed and becomes valid. It is a grave and often costly mistake for a seller to become involved in purchasing another home or leasing an apartment on the strength of his executed contract alone. One must provide that any future commitment be contingent upon the *closing* of a present home on or about a specified date. Many wishful-thinking sellers assume an executed contract is a closed sale, completely forgetting the real estate axiom which says: "A sale is not closed until all of the checks from the sale have been deposited and cleared." Therefore, any legal commitments to purchase or lease, or otherwise become involved as a result of selling the home, should provide a legal escape clause if, for any reason, the anticipated sale does not go through. This applies as well to selling household furnishings and other valuables. This precaution is routine advice from every attorney, but quite often sellers do not seek it before they leap.

### More Buyers

It always happens! A seller waits for weeks—sometimes months—for the right anxious buyer or the return of the couple who looked "just right for our house." However, the day after the contract is signed, the phone calls start coming in fast and furiously from realtors, pre-contract-signing lookers, and the neighbors next door—all wanting to buy. If this happens to you (and it probably will), do not advise callers that your home is sold. At this point it is not!

Leave the door open by asking if they wish to make a legal commitment to purchase in the event that, for any reason, the present contract for sale does not result in a favorable closing. Seek the advice of your attorney for guidance as to how to proceed in pinning down a good "just in case" backup prospect or prospects. It is not uncommon for a seller to have two or more contracts for sale in the works at the same time, providing they are in proper sequence of preference and within a reasonable time frame. This enviable position gives you the opportunity, in the event the contract of the first sale does not go through, to automatically make contract two the prime and enforceable contract. The pressure on the first buyer to expedite and appreciate the opportunity of purchasing your home is increased, knowing there are others in the wings with more than conversation on their minds. However, it never pays to take a smug position, just because you have one executed contract and others who say they want to be called immediately if the present sale does not go through. If they are *really* that serious, they will be prepared to do more than leave you or the realtor their phone number.

You are obligated, both morally and legally, to advise all listing real estate brokers of your contract status—this should be done immediately, preferably by mail. Tell them that though your home is under contract, you would entertain the contingency-type contract discussed above.

### Closing Date, Time, and Place

Most contracts for sale state a specific closing date, time, and place. Although specified in the contract, and anticipated at its inception, rarely is the transaction closed on that date for any of a dozen reasons. Once most of the contingencies on which the contract is based have been met and it appears that all is well, the real estate office and attorneys involved in the transaction begin the process of scheduling the actual closing. This is as difficult as trying to get a definite commitment from ten people to join you for dinner and a show a week from Saturday at 6:00 P.M.

Setting up the closing is the responsibility of the brokerage firm representing the seller. The closing usually takes place at the office of the lending institution extending mortgage financing to the buyer. Those in attendance at the average closing are the sellers, the buyers and their respective attorneys, the title company representative, an officer of the financing institution, the real estate representatives involved with the transaction, and those who must be personally present to execute releases of any liens filed against the property, such as federal and state tax agents. The juggling process required to meet schedules and prior commitments of all these individuals should be accomplished at least two weeks prior to the formal closing, and then reconfirmed two days before the big event. Once you have been advised of the date, time, and place, it's worthwhile for *you* to personally reconfirm, so as to avoid any last minute mix-ups that often happen and mean rescheduling once again. Contact your attorney a few days prior to closing, so that you may be fully prepared to bring any documents, checks, or other important materials with you.

### Don't Overlook

Once you have been notified of the exact closing date, don't forget to do any number of the following:

- Fill out a change of address form at the post office.
- Leave a note for your milkman.
- Prepare photocopies of old deeds, documents, photographs, clippings, *etc.* for presentation to the buyers. Many buyers are very interested in the history of the property.
- Notify the paper boy or girl.
- Confirm your moving plans with your mover.
- Take necessary procedures to terminate all utilities; but, to avoid interruption of service, do not do so until you coordinate your plans with your buyer's.
- Have a conference with your insurance agent, but do not cancel formally until the closing has actually taken place and arrangements have been made for the coverage of items not being sold. Discuss the status of personal liability coverage once the sale has been closed.
- Terminate any routine personal service relationships, such as with gardeners, window cleaners, a cleaning service, and so on. Put them in contact with the new owners if their service has been satisfactory.

- Remove the three cartons of old family photographs still in the attic.
- Obtain all necessary forms and instructions to comply with laws and regulations for the licensing of autos, professions, and dogs.
- Repair or replace whatever you promised the buyers you would.
- Clean up. Buyers expect your home to be spotless the day they move in—will they be disappointed?
- Organize and label all keys to take with you to the closing for presentation to the buyers. Have extras made if they are lost or do not fit properly.
- Label your fuse box or circuit breaker if it is not clearly marked.
- Invite the new buyers to spend a few hours with you for instructions—for example, where to kick the dishwasher if it should suddenly shut off.
- Make a list of the things you don't wish to overlook.

The importance of frequent contact during the period from contract to closing with the key people—attorney, realtor, and buyer—cannot be overemphasized. Any breakdown in communications during this crucial period of your sale might unreasonably delay the closing or void the contract. Your interest will be appreciated, welcomed, and best served by staying close to the scene.

# 11

## *Reducing Closing Costs*

The purpose of this chapter is to alert you to the various costs and expenses normally attributable to the seller that must be paid at the time of closing. There are certain fixed charges, set either by law or by custom, and there are those subject to the negotiations and presale understanding, which could result in meaningful savings to you.

The following schedule of closing costs outlines what they are and how to cope with them.

*Legal Fees:* Selecting an attorney to represent you from inception to closing should not be done on the basis of cost. Much depends upon the experience, competence, and overall ability of counsel you select to best protect your interests in making the deal and avoiding breaking it.

Several chapters in this book emphasize the importance of getting your act together prior to formal listing, so as to eliminate clostly delays and possible loss of sale. Therefore, if you do your homework well and have all of your documents and related material in order, you can then expect your legal fees to be substantially reduced, in contrast to those homeowners who dump the mess on the lawyer's desk.

If you have had a family attorney for many years who is familiar with your home, estate, tax status, attitude, and personality, and you have been comfortable and satisfied with past services, then I certainly would recommend you continue accordingly. Asking what the fee will be clears the air, and most attorneys welcome this inquiry, although some are shy and reluctant to initiate the discussion. Fee-setting policies of attorneys in a real estate transaction vary from a percentage of the sale price to a minimum fee plus a per-hour charge and expenses. There are, of course, several exceptions to these two most common fee formulas.

If the selecting of an attorney presents a dilemma because you are not familiar with any in your area, ask your bank, local bar association, or real estate board to supply you with the names of three attorneys or law firms well experienced in real estate matters. At that point, it is worth the effort for you to determine the anticipated fee from those recommended.

You might want to consider during the negotiating process with a prospective buyer, or in the listing of details of your home, that the fees for your attorney be the responsibility of the purchaser, either in part or full. This may save you several hundred dollars or more at the time of closing. Besides, it is not uncommon for a sales contract to state that attorney's fees, brokerage commissions, and survey costs, usually applicable to the seller, will be the obligation of the buyer.

Under no circumstances, however, should one attorney represent both buyer and seller. Most attorneys will not put themselves in this precarious position, even though they have permission of both parties and the total cost would probably be less than representation by individual counsel.

***Real Estate Broker's Commission:*** The day of closing is *not* the time to negotiate the amount of commission payable to the broker. A brokerage fee from 5 percent to 10 percent of the sale price varies throughout the country and is normally established between owner and broker at the time of listing. The amount of brokerage commission is not generally established or fixed by law; therefore, you are in a position to establish as a condition of listing either a percentage of sale price or a flat fee.

You will note in Chapter 6, "Finding the Indispensable Broker/Realtor," the many considerations other than fee that the seller must take into account when selecting an exclusive agent for representation or offering the property to several firms on an "open" basis. You can reduce this major closing-cost item by:

- negotiating on a flat fee basis;
- reducing the negotiated fee if your selling price is reduced;
- or making periodic payments instead of one lump sum at closing, if you hold the mortgage, with such periodic payments contingent upon the buyer meeting mortgage obligations on time.

If your home and general economic conditions warrant, you might want to consider asking several leading brokerage firms to submit bids for listing your home. You may be pleasantly surprised with the results. It is worth repeating here that you should not make your selection solely on the basis of fee, but should select only the well-established, aggressive, active, and reliable broker or firm.

*Recording Fees:* This cost is usually under $25 and is a fixed charge for various documents to be put on record, such as the satisfaction of your mortgage and releases of various obligations, such as leases, judgments, *etc.*

*Transfer Fees:* These amounts will vary widely from one state to another throughout the country. The seller is obligated to pay various fees, stamps, or miscellaneous charges, based upon a nominal percentage of the sale price of the property, involved mortgage, if any, and personal property evaluation being transferred. The amount of this classification in most states, for the sale of less than $100,000, would probably be no less than $100, but no more than $200.

*Mortgage Points:* Certain federal- and state-sponsored mortgage plans, such as G.I., F.H.A., and local authority financing, require the seller to pay the lending institution a nominal percentage of the mortgage granted the buyer. If this point system is in effect, the purchaser is obligated to pay most of the one-time charge involved. Each point is 1 percent of the total amount of mortgage granted. Example: A mortgage in the amount of $50,000 with a three-point charge would be $1500 (3 percent x $50,000). The purchaser might be obligated to pay two points and the seller one point or, in this example, the seller would be obligated to pay $500. In a tight mortgage-market situation, the point system may apply to conventional lending institutions and regular mortgages, providing state law permits the procedure. It is important that you are aware in advance of signing your contract of this obligation prior to closing, and that you try to save this hefty charge by negotiating your sale price accordingly or by making other adjustments, providing there are no laws to the contrary.

*Rentals:* Any rentals you have received from part or all of your property, paid in advance to you for the period beyond the closing date, are normally refunded to the new owner. This adjustment does not necessarily have to be made, providing you make it known what portion of the prepayment is not to be refunded as part of the sale. A reasonable rental is usually charged the seller in the event the seller occupies all or part of the premises sold beyond the closing date and does not give full possession to the buyer. Try to avoid occupancy beyond the closing date at any expense but, if you must, it is not unreasonable to occupy free of charge for a period of less than a month.

*Title Guarantee Policy:* If you are selling your home in an area where it is customary for the seller to provide an up-to-date title search or title guarantee policy, you might save some money by asking the buyer to assume part or all of the cost as a condition of sale. Check with your attorney as to the cost involved and guide yourself accordingly.

## Important Points to Remember

To help reduce closing costs that are impossible to avoid or adjust, do not overlook obtaining payment for the following items at the day of closing:

- Reimbursement from the buyer of all general property taxes paid in advance for the period beyond the date of closing
- Cost of oil, coal, or other fuel on hand at the current market price as of closing day
- Refund of all prepaid insurance premiums
- Prepaid service contracts which will remain in force beyond the closing date
- Balance in the escrow account in the bank holding your mortgage
- Return of all water, gas, electric, telephone, and other utility deposits held by applicable companies
- Refund of any interest paid on the mortgage in advance of the closing date
- Balance due for any personal property the purchaser agreed to buy but did not include in the contract
- Any sales taxes due from the buyer where state and local provisions make the seller responsible for filing a return and paying the tax.

Closing costs are a necessary evil involved in the sale of a home. A substantial sum of money is involved and often overlooked in the excitement and trauma surrounding the sale of the residence. By anticipating the day of reckoning, the seller will be able to save.

Before making that final commitment to sell and agreeing to price, be well aware of all closing costs and don't forget the net proceeds from the sale will be reduced by the amount of your outstanding mortgage balance, whether it is assumed by the buyer or paid the day of closing. Ask your attorney and/or broker to provide a detailed statement of closing costs well in advance. This will set the record straight and eliminate any shocks or surprises.

# 12

## *Avoiding the Income Tax Bite*

Selling your home *for* Top Dollar is one thing—keeping that money is another. Recent tax legislation aimed at giving the seller a break might prove a bonanza if your sale is structured properly. The income tax consequences resulting from the sale of a home must be considered and evaluated *before* and not *after* the sale, a lesson some Top Dollar sellers wish they had learned prior to listing. Before formally placing your home on the market, income tax counseling with your tax adviser, CPA, and/or attorney might result in a saving of thousands of dollars in federal, state, and local income taxes. The wording of a contract of sale, the date of closing, other income and losses, marital status, your future home plans, your age and your spouse's, and the original cost and improvements of the home being sold are but a few of the vital considerations that have major income tax ramifications. Once your home is sold, the horse is out of the barn—it's too late then to mend the fences.

It will be necessary for you to do some homework prior to making an appointment with the experts. Certain tabulations and research are prerequisites to a professional review of your status. The primary objective is to determine, in accordance with Internal Revenue Service regulations, how much profit you will be making by selling your home; what portion of the profit, if any, is taxable; and what you can do, legally, to reduce or avoid paying the tax on that profit.

You can well imagine that computing your profit is a bit more complicated than subtracting the price you paid for your home from the eventual selling price. If you purchased your home, the original cost used for computing gain is not simply the original purchase price; it is that original cost *plus* certain closing costs at that time *plus* major improvements since acquisition *plus* the sprucing-up expenditures prior to sale *plus* your agent's brokerage fee and your attorney's fee for the sale. If you acquired the home now being sold as a gift, an inheritance, or as part of a divorce settlement or you constructed it yourself, your basis for computing gain on sale is another seminar.

It is my intention to provide you with sufficient information in this chapter so that you may be well aware of the income tax savings available to a home seller. I have incorporated the highlights of my discussions with prominent certified public accountants and attorneys, who generally acknowledged that a substantial number of homeowners retain their services *after* they have sold their homes. In many of these cases, these homeowner clients could have avoided major tax liabilities through a consultation prior to contract signing.

It will prove helpful for you to review the following definitions of the terms used in the foreign language known as Income Tax Law.

*Basis of Determing Gain or Loss:* The amount, computed in accordance with tax regulations, that will be the figure subtracted from the selling price of the home to determine gain or loss on sale.

*Selling Price:* The total amount agreed to between buyer and seller, normally referred to as the total consideration for the transfer. For income tax purposes, the selling price includes not only cash received but also such items as the mortgage assumed by the buyer, notes in lieu of cash, and other valuable considerations.

*Expense of Sale:* Cost directly attributable to the sale of the home and paid by the seller—for example, real estate brokerage commissions; lawyers' fees; miscellaneous fees and services; recording and transfer fees; bank and finance charges; fixing-up expenses incurred primarily in anticipation of sale (including painting and decorating), which must have been completed ninety days prior to contract to qualify; and other general cosmetic improvements.

*Principal Residence:* For most taxpayers, the home they live in is their principal residence. For those who maintain more than one living unit, the determination, for tax purposes, of what is the principal residence is not easily reached. Factors considered in determining principal-residence status are: place of voting; address most commonly used for mail or filing of tax returns; registration of automobiles; physical presence; and employment status. An apartment in the city in which you work might be considered your principal residence even though you own a home in the suburbs or country that you occupy part time. Legally, and for tax purposes, it is important for you to establish your principal-residence status well in advance of selling what you might *think* is your principal residence. There have been many tax-court cases wherein the Internal Revenue Service disallowed favorable provisions for the sale of principal residence of the taxpayer. Most of the liberal tax breaks for the sale of a home apply to the sale of the principal residence only —not the one you choose as such, but the one established as such from the facts of your individual situation.

*Installment Sale of Principal Residence:* This provision enables the seller of a principal residence to pay the tax on the gain of the sale over the years of collection from the buyer instead of making a full payment in the year of sale. The right to elect to defer the tax liability under this provision is available providing the seller limits payments on principal received from the buyer to 30 percent or less of the selling price in the year of sale.

*Day of Sale:* For tax purposes, this is either the date of closing or the date title (deed) to the property passes from the seller to the buyer.

*Capital Gain:* The taxable portion on the *gain* of a sale of a principal residence, limited to only 40 percent of the total gain. Assuming your gain is $50,000, only $20,000 (40 percent) of the $50,000 will be taxable. The actual tax you pay on this $20,000 will vary, depending upon your other income and deductions.

Discuss with your tax advisers the following provisions in the tax law and how you may best take advantage of the savings they provide:

1.    Any amount of gain up to a maximum of $100,000 is tax-free providing:

a) ownership of the home is in joint names, and either spouse was fifty-five years of age or older *prior* to the date of closing. If title to the property being sold is in one spouse's name only, that spouse must be fifty-five or older on the date of closing to qualify under this provision.

b) owners have occupied the principal residence for at least three years during the five years preceding the date of closing. A more liberal time period is available to those over sixty-five at the day of closing; this is applicable to sale prior to July 25, 1981.

(This up-to-$100,000 tax-free benefit may only be used once in a lifetime.)

2.    If you sell your principal residence at a gain, you have the option of not paying tax on the gain at this time, providing:

a) you purchase another principal residence for a price equal to or exceeding the selling price of your present principal residence. This acquisition must be made within eighteen months before or after the closing date of your home sale. Principal residence is not limited to same type of home—it could be a co-op apartment, condominium, or houseboat.

b) you are constructing a new home as principal residence, in which case the time limit may be extended. Consult with a tax adviser about this provision.

(If only a portion of the total selling price is reinvested in a new principal residence, only a portion of total gain may be nontaxable at the time.)

3.  Homeowners anticipating a substantial gain on the sale of their principal residence might consider selling other capital assets, such as stocks and securities, on which a substantial loss would be realized. Taking the loss at this time would offset all or part of the gain from the sale of the residence, reducing or eliminating the tax liability attributable to the home sale. For example: A company's stock was purchased for $50,000 and now has a market value of $20,000. If sold, it would result in a loss of $30,000. The sale of a principal residence which realizes a gain of $30,000 would be totally offset by the loss on the sale of stocks, thus eliminating any tax liability from the gain on the home sale.

4.  Check with your tax adviser or attorney for information pertaining to:
    • the tax-saving possibilities in trading or exchanging your principal residence, as opposed to selling it.
    • donating part or all of your principal residence to charitable institutions recognized by the Internal Revenue Service.

- giving gifts to members of your family in anticipation of a sale.
- the effect of the sale of a residence on other income and estate taxes.

5.  The installment sale provision allows the seller to report the gain on the sale of a home over the period of years the sum is collected from the buyer. This is most applicable where the seller takes back his mortgage as a substantial payment for the home. The following conditions must be met to qualify under this section:

a) The taxpayer must not receive more than 30 percent of the selling price *in the year of sale* from proceeds of the down payment and any subsequent principal payments received within that year.

b) If more than 30 percent of the selling price is received in the year of sale, the taxpayer is required to pay tax on the entire gain from the sale of the home even though only a portion of the sale price was received.

c) Receiving more than 30 percent is considered a closed sale, as if all monies were received. Mortgage interest received in the year of sale is *not* considered in the 30-percent-or-less computation.

(This provision is available to sellers of both principal and nonprincipal residences.)

If you are selling your principal residence as one unit along with other land or buildings *not* used as part of your principal residence—such as a farm, retail outlet, professional office, kennel, stable, drive-in facility, studio, manufacturing plant or the like—you can still take advantage of the tax benefits provided under the principal-residence sale. This is accomplished by apportioning the total selling price between the land and building used as principal residence and that which is not. Consult with your attorney and tax adviser prior to making a firm commitment, and certainly before executing a contract of sale, to determine the most advantageous procedure to follow, producing the best tax result. Many attorneys representing sellers have insisted that two separate contracts and deeds be prepared and executed where the sale of one parcel consists of both the principal residence and other nonqualifying types of property. This documentation clearly separates for income-tax-audit review one potentially nontaxable portion from the other. Allocation of each is clearly substantiated by the formal appraisal of a qualified expert and is not arbitrarily apportioned solely for the purpose of providing the best tax advantage.

If you occupy part of a multifamily home owned as your primary residence and rent or lease the rest of it, the tax provisions available in the case of a sale of the principal residence are also available to you by the allocation method. Assume you own a three-family home and occupy one-third as your principal residence, with the other two-thirds consisting of rented apartments. You sell the entire home for $90,000. You would then report the sale of your principal residence at $30,000 (one-third of $90,000), under the same procedure you would have used had you sold a single-family home for $30,000. You would, of course, have to compute your gain on a pro-rata basis.

Homeowners who elect to defer payment of tax on the gain from the sale of a home by reinvesting the proceeds of the sale in another principal residence must keep in mind that, for tax purposes, the cost of the replacement home is reduced by the amount of gain on which tax was deferred. For example: The present home is being sold for $100,000, on which there is a gain of $60,000, and the replacement home costs $110,000. There is no tax payable at this time under the deferment provision. When and if the replacement home is sold, the cost basis is not $110,000 but $50,000 ($110,000 minus the $60,000 gain deferred). Assume further that the replacement home was sold for

$110,000. The gain would then be $60,000, unless you took advantage of one or more special provisions applicable at that time which would either reduce, defer, or eliminate the tax.

As discussed in Chapter 9, homeowners frequently sell their homes with all or part of their furnishings—personal property- —in a lump-sum deal. This is fine for sale purposes, but it might result in adverse income tax consequences, particularly if the personal property included in the sale has a market value in excess of a few thousand dollars. Some of the liberal tax advantages available to those selling their principal residence apply only to real property—land, buildings, and fixtures. The sale of personal property comes under other provisions and must not be included in the sale price when that is reported for tax purposes. State- and local-sales-tax offices are also interested in the sale of personal property. Making a reasonable allocation between real property and personal property is advised prior to a sale commitment and final negotiations.

The installment method of reporting gain on the sale of a home is a primary benefit to the following categories of sellers:

- Those not eligible to take advantage of the one-time $100,000 gain provision due to age or principal-residence requirements.
- Those who do not plan to purchase or build a replacement principal residence within the time period allotted.
- Those who must provide 70 percent or more of the primary financing needed by a Top Dollar buyer due to a shortage of institutional mortgage financing or other reasons.
- Those with other substantial capital gains and ordinary income in the year of the sale of the home but who anticipate that the other income will be greatly reduced in coming years. (A lower income means a lower income tax bracket.)
- Those who anticipate a hefty gain from the sale of a home.

The basic concept of the installment-reporting provision gives the taxpayer the opportunity of limiting the tax payment on the gain of sale of the home to that portion of the total that is received each year. It further provides the advantage of reporting the pro-rata gain in years when the taxpayer's other income is nominal and when exemptions for age and other benefits are applicable and may provide an attractive minimum-risk investment. (Not all divisions of government levying an income tax conform to federal provisions; therefore it is mandatory that you engage in tax consultation prior to contract commitment. What may be fully exempt on the federal return may be fully taxable by the state or vice versa.)

Here are a few actual case histories involving people (the names have been changed to protect the born-again taxpayer) who sold their principal residences without obtaining and following professional tax guidance:

♠ Mr. and Mrs. Fred Ames entered into a contract in February to sell their home, purchased thirty years ago for $75,000, for $185,000. The closing took place in April. Mr. Ames turned fifty-five in November of the same year. He assumed that the first $100,000 of the $110,000 gain ($185,000 minus $75,000) was tax-free under the one-time $100,000 tax provision. He further assumed that this provision was available to the home owner/taxpayer, providing the fifty-five-years-of-age-or-over provision was met at any time prior to the year end in which the sale was made and not at the time of the actual closing. He regretfully learned, when filing his income tax return, that had he delayed closing until after November, he would have been $20,000 richer. Note: Title to the property was in both names, but Mrs. Ames was only fifty-one years old.

♠ Jane Finley, age twenty-eight, sold her principal residence in Connecticut for $92,000. Her tax adviser computed her gain as $26,000 and advised her that she could defer paying tax on that gain providing she purchased another residence at her new place of employment in California within eighteen months, computed from the day of closing the sale on her home. The sale and gain were reported on her timely income tax return, along with the memo stating that she planned to invest in another principal residence within one year and therefore did not pay any tax on that transaction. Jane moved to California and decided to rent an attractive apartment under a one-year lease, during which time she would be looking for a home. She became discouraged with the availability of homes in her price range and renewed her lease, after the first year's expiration, for an additional year. A few months after the eighteen-month time provision had elapsed, she found exactly the home she wanted and made the purchase. She had completely forgotten the replacement-home provision until the day she received a bill from the Internal Revenue Service for $2,500, the tax due on the sale of her home in Connecticut.

♠ Mr. and Mrs. Warren Howard, a professional couple who devote an average of three days a week as advertising executive and designer in a major city, maintain a sizeable rented apartment near their metropolitan offices. Approximately twenty years ago, they purchased a large home fifty miles from the city, where they reside when not working in the city. As a matter of convenience and comfortable routine, all mail is directed to their city apartment and they use the city address on their tax returns, licenses, applications, and subscriptions—not giving any particular attention to the principal-residence status as defined in the Internal Revenue Code.

They decided to sell their home in the suburbs, anticipating an expansion of their city activities. The sale of their home was consummated within a few months for $160,000, resulting in a gain of $90,000 (cost basis: $70,000). Mr. Howard, age fifty-seven, did not anticipate any income tax liability on the sale, as he took the one-time up-to-$100,000 exemption applicable under the prevailing law. The Howards reported the sale on their income tax return and claimed the suburban home as their principal residence for tax purposes.

The Internal Revenue Service disallowed the exemption on the basis that the principal residence of the Howards was the city apartment and not the home that was sold. The government issued a bill for $18,000, plus interest of $1,100. The taxpayers took the case to the tax courts and the issue was decided in favor of the IRS. The government based its case on the fact that the Howards could not prove or document by the evidence submitted that the suburban home was their principal residence, even though they spent more time away from the city than in their apartment.

♠ Mrs. Helen Stokes occupied her home, purchased originally for $14,000, as a principal residence for over twenty years. She made substantial improvments for ten years after acquisition. Due to health reasons, she sold her home and went to live with her son and daughter-in-law.

Her tax adviser asked her to supply him with the original home cost information and evidence of all improvements made from the time of purchase to determine the gain on the sale of the home. She was unable to provide canceled checks or bills for most of the improvements, as some were discarded in the moving process and others were never saved. She estimated that the improvements made after acquisition amounted to more than $30,000. These improvements plus the original cost ($30,000 plus $14,000) totaled $44,000. The sale price after expenses of the sale was $74,000, resulting in a gain of $30,000.

Mrs. Stokes, at age fifty-one, did not qualify for the one-time exemption or replacement provisions for tax exemption of gain. It was therefore necessary to document her cost basis and improvements in an effort to reduce the gain as much as possible. She and her family were advised by her tax consultant to reconstruct from memory and physical inspection reasonable estimates of the improvements made. This was done by contacting the various suppliers, contractors, and service firms who had performed the tasks. The effort proved 75 percent successful, an above-average accomplishment because of the time lapse involved. In the event of an audit of her return, she was told that a portion of the 25 percent not documented might be disallowed in computing the gain.

▲ Jack and Ida Wise agreed to sell their 125-acre estate home for $325,000, of which the buyers would pay $125,000 at closing and the Wise couple would provide $200,000 as mortgage financing (purchase-money mortgage). The mortgage term was for ten years at $10^{1}/_{4}$ percent, to be amortized monthly. The terms and conditions of the sale were negotiated and agreed upon without any consultation by the Wises with their attorney or accountant. They were so pleased to have sold their home at near asking price that they gave little or no consideration to the tax consequences of their anticipated gain of well over $175,000.

Had they structured their sale under the installment-reporting method and taken $95,000 or less, instead of $125,000, for down payment, they would have saved thousands of dollars in federal and state income taxes. By taking a down payment of more than 30 percent of the selling price in the year of sale, they were obligated to report the gain as if they had received the entire proceeds of the sale at closing.

For those of you who acquired homes by purchase, it will be necessary to provide your tax adviser with the following detailed information:

- The original cost of your home and the date it was acquired.
- Dates of birth of you and your spouse.
- Closing costs at the time of purchase—such as attorneys' fees, title policy/search, recording and miscellaneous fees, and other costs not previously deductible.

- All improvements made since acquisition, identifying the improvement, the approximate date, and the cost. Do not overlook cost of shrubbery, the new heating system, driveways, additions, the new roof, air conditioning, garages, basement improvements, water softeners, new wells, septics, and plumbing improvements.
- Copies of the last four years' income tax returns. They might provide the basis for income-averaging provisions for tax savings.
- Some evidence to establish actual residence in the home being sold.
- Any information relating to the sale of a previous principal residence, regardless of when it was sold.
- Evidence of title (ownership), reflected in the existing deed or deeds.
- Schedule of the current year's anticipated income from all sources.
- Schedule of the current year's major expenditures.
- Schedule of all anticipated closing costs associated with the sale of your principal residence.

If the residence being sold was not acquired by purchase, provide all details of acquisition such as gift tax returns, wills, estate-tax information returns, and separation-or-divorce-decree agreements.

Every administration since the inception of the income tax system in 1913 has promised the American taxpayer a simplification of the income tax laws. Tax law is now so voluminous and complex that it is hardly possible to get a clear-cut answer to most provisions of the tax codes. One thing is certain—the sale of your home, whether for $30,000 or $3 million, is going to have *some* income tax ramifications. It is prudent to be conscious that there will always be an April 15. Only a thorough analysis of your situation with your tax adviser will reveal the best plan to follow. Any one of the provisions listed in this chapter might be to your advantage, and a combination of two or more could reduce or eliminate your tax.

But remember, just because the federal government has taken some of the tax burden away from the sale of a primary residence, particularly for those of you more than fifty-five years of age, don't let this dissuade you from getting involved, if need be, in the financing of your sale. In other words, just because there is no longer any incentive to taking back a good portion of the sale price (as either a first or second mortgage) and spreading that income over a several year period in order to avoid the tax bite, you shouldn't hesitate to still do so. After all, if you don't, there may be no sale at all, therefore no tax.

# III

# *Ruling the Exception or What to Do with That Unique Property*

# 13

## *Selling Your Second Home*

Great numbers of Americans own a country home, a lake cottage or a mountain lodge—a home away from home, purchased primarily for recreation, escape from the cities, or investment. For the past twenty years, interest in being a two-home family has set a pattern for the affluent American comparable to the earlier goal of a two-car garage. Changing economic and personal cycles affect great numbers of second-home owners across the country, however; and it is to those wishing to sell these second homes that this chapter is dedicated.

To achieve Top Dollar results from this category, most of the advice and procedures offered throughout this book apply, but with differences unique to country and shore property. Remember, these considerations are *in addition* to previously detailed information.

### Country-Home Property

One of the primary concerns of those seeking country property in the 1980s will be the amount of land (acreage) surrounding the home. The country buyer wants land for investment, protection, privacy, and some agricultural value potential. The interest in space for horses for breeding or recreation, vineyards, orchards, forest plantations, and vegetable gardens equals or exceeds interest in the home itself. This was not true ten or fifteen years ago. Also, the energy crunch has caused a dramatic increase in the demand for country places with a woodlot sufficient to meet primary or auxiliary heating needs. But it has also frightened some people away from the thought of a country home. That's why, if you live in an area that has been hard hit by gasoline shortages, you might think about installing a 500- to 2,000-gallon tank with a hand pump, where local zoning permits, and ask a local distributor to fill it with regular gas or diesel fuel.

In general, however, the ideal country property is one that can be offered with a balance of land consisting of open or cleared acreage, wooded areas, grazing or agricultural space with good access, reasonable topography, quiet, public road frontage, and pastoral views. Everyone who wants country wants water—stream, pond, or brook. The emphasis on the land and the balance desired does not necessarily mean that a hundred or more acres are required to satisfy Top Dollar buyers. Reasonable balance may be achieved on a five- to ten-acre country property, and no balance at all on one with two hundred acres. The goal is to supply the important criteria of would-be buyers within the confines of the acreage owned.

The present country-place owner is in an enviable position if the property can reasonably match what the buyer of today and tomorrow will seek. It is to those owners who fall short of the important demands that I offer the following suggestions:

- Contact your local office of the United States Agricultural Stabilization and Conservation Services. They will provide a wide range of free and invaluable advice in reference to water potential (such as ponds and other watersheds); soil testing; land use; crop, orchard, or vineyard information; flood control; forestry programs; and a broad overview of how best to make use of the land you own to achieve your personal goals.

- Call your regional state office of agricultural conservation for additional information relative to programs related to your acreage.
- Obtain serious estimates of costs for land clearance, agricultural plantings, pond construction, and related projects.
- If your acreage is limited (under ten acres), or does not lend itself to creating a balance of land use, consider purchasing adjoining or contiguous acreage—providing this additional investment will result in a more attractive land package and will enhance the value of your home and buildings.
- If you wish to limit your investment in additional land or are not interested in purchasing, for whatever personal or financial reason, try to obtain an option (right to buy) for any land contiguous to or across the road from your property. Consult with your attorney in reference to the suggested option, which is a legal document giving you the absolute right to purchase the described property for a specified sum within an agreed-upon time period. It is to your advantage to have as long a period as possible, but settle for as little as sixty or ninety days if the owner will agree. The purpose of obtaining the option is to attract a purchaser who may be satisfied with your primary home, buildings, location, asking price, *etc.* but will only buy providing more land is available. If you are in a position to have additional land readily available, it could very well be the difference between Top Dollar sale of your present country property or losing a prime opportunity to sell. Owners of adjoining property are somewhat reluctant to tie up their land for a reasonable time by giving an option to strangers, but, if you proceed as a neighbor, chances are good that the response will be neighborly. You might even offer to pay the adjoining property owner something for the privilege

of obtaining such an option, or be prepared to pay any reasonable sum he requests.

• Consult with several leading real estate firms specializing in the sale of country property in your area and ask them the following question: "What should I do, in order of priority, to make this property the most attractive of all available in this price category to the best clients you now have in your office, or who will walk in your door?" Be sure to emphasize you wish an overview. Their concentration should not be solely on the home or buildings, but on *all* aspects of your property. No one will ask you to move a mountain, but you might have a path cleared so someone can get to the top of it.

Buildings, barns, and other living accommodations in addition to the primary country home are extremely important to those seeking country property. Do not neglect to keep all structures in good condition and to perk them up, if needed, prior to listing your property for sale. Give some consideration to making a small investment in creating a few stables for horses or a modest apartment above a garage or in a small barn, or building a working studio or office with a skylight, if needed. You might be occupying your country home on a full-time basis, but keep in mind that thousands of country homes are weekend retreats where owners will want accommodations for caretakers or good tenants for security and other purposes. An expenditure of less than $15,000, to expand the market potential to those willing and able to pay for it, will enhance the value of your basic offering.

If you have any land that has been lying dormant and is suitable for agricultural purposes, spare no effort to make it look alive and well by renting or giving this land to a neighboring farmer for a limited time. Most buyers will not object to this arrangement but will probably continue with the present farmer after their purchase.

Do not neglect any existing fencing. This is an important factor for the animal-oriented buyer. Also, have a professional cultivate, spray, and prune orchards, vineyards, and the rest surrounding the *House and Garden* main home. Few other small investments will contribute so much to the top asking price and the beauty of the country.

Those paying the highest prices for country places are those who spend most of their working week in the city.

To them, "Country" is not only a place a hundred miles away from the hub-bub of the city, but a place where there are animals, trees, and lots of green crops, and ponds are spring-fed with unpolluted water. The world they are willing to pay well for is a comfortable place that is quiet and peaceful and does not remind them in any way of the world they leave behind Friday afternoon, even though it may be the best the city can provide.

Reflect on *your* reasons for going to the country. Today reasons are basically the same, but prices have soared to the point where only the most affluent are able to afford the fulfillment of "country."

Preparing your place for sale with these thoughts in mind will aid in fulfilling their needs and your goal—Top Dollar sale.

## The Home at the Shore

From Cape Cod to Malibu, the magnetic attraction of the ocean continues to draw record numbers seeking a home at the shore. No longer is the seasonal or weekend home on or near the beach being purchased for the typical one-purpose use. Aspiring owners of today are offered an attractive investment for part- or full-time rental, as well as the opportunity to convert to year-round use as a permanent home—plus a good hedge against inflation.

For many years, owners of shore property took their places in the sun for granted and generally did the minimum of repair and maintenance, particularly those owners who only occupied their homes during the few summer months. Over a period of a few years, the homes were battered and showed signs of neglect, but they continued to serve a limited purpose to the owners. The past five years have demonstrated a strong existing market for shore homes. Those of you who wish to reap the harvest of this intense interest might consider the following suggestions to achieve Top Dollar results:

- Review your present structure with an architect and/or contractor to obtain cost estimates to convert from part-time or limited use to year-round occupancy. Particular emphasis should be directed to the installation of an adequate heating system, insulation, and a wood-burning stove or fireplace; enlarging the kitchen; and the like. Once an estimate has been obtained, you will have to decide, possibly with the aid of professional assistance, whether the projected investment to update and convert will be justified by a top resale price and probable marketability. Over the past few years, many owners of shore property have found that an investment not exceeding $30,000 brought an excellent return from seasonal or year-round rentals to responsible tenants. Some owners have met with success by offering the tenants the opportunity to rent with an option to buy, crediting all or a portion of the rental toward an agreed selling price.

- Consult with neighboring owners who might share similar sale goals in an effort to take advantage of joint improvement services. In this way you can reduce the individual cost by having several jobs undertaken at the same time by one or a few contractors. This will also create a much improved image of the immediate area to prospective buyers and investors.

- Try to eliminate the usual anxieties of shore-property purchasers by improving or constructing jetties or breakwaters, shoring up bulkheads, planting beach grass to reduce erosion, and pinning down good insurance coverage.

- Furnish your home tastefully with a modest number of comfortable and functional furnishings. Offering the home for sale furnished does have a special attraction to most shore-home buyers.
- If the size of your land plot is small, or your access to the beach area is limited, try to obtain an option to purchase adjoining property. This will prove helpful in negotiating with prospective purchasers who find your home desirable and attractive but wish to expand or require more elbow room.
- Do not limit your marketing effort to local brokers nor to a particular time of year. Major sales are accomplished on a year-round basis, contrary to the opinion of many that the best time to sell is at the time of year when the property shows best.
- Group purchasing is quite common now for shore property, so do not be reluctant to negotiate accordingly.
- If you are reluctant to make any substantial investment for improvement and updating, consider a lease arrangement with a responsible person or persons at less than the going rental. Do this providing the tenant or tenants will undertake a series of improvements at their own cost and expense, and offer them an option to buy at Top Dollar.

Cost of approved building sites near or on the shore is rapidly becoming prohibitive, and availability is scarce in the most popular shore areas throughout the country. The value of a site with good water and sewage-disposal systems has, in many instances, become more valuable than the structure located thereon. Do not overlook this fact when pricing the property. Consider what comparable available sites are selling for without any structure or underground utilities, when establishing the value of your total property. Having a home at the shore is indeed a valuable asset, and all reasonable projections for its increase in value are excellent.

Sellers of second homes no longer have to look exclusively for buyers from what has been known as the "second-home market." During the past few years, a substantial percentage of country and shore homes have been sold to local purchasers for permanent occupancy. With the cost of building sites and new construction skyrocketing, owners of second homes are finding a lively market in their own backyard.

# 14

## *Did George Washington Sleep Here?*

Today more and more people are uncovering unbelievable fortunes in their attics: old paintings, furniture, clothing, books, and coins. And yet sometimes it is the attic itself that represents untold value, especially for the home seller.

That is, many people are discovering that their home, because of its age or perhaps some historical value, is eligible for listing in the *National Register of Historic Places.* What's more, eligibility has absolutely nothing to do with the size of the place —it could even be that old hand-hewn, post-and-beam barn or stone smokehouse out back—or its condition. No, you needn't pour a million dollars into your home to qualify, for the *National Register* is not a special privilege for the Super Rich.

Maybe that's why the demand for historic, antique homes is taking its place alongside the unprecedented interest in early American art, furniture, and other eighteenth- and nineteenth-century authentic collectibles. In fact, sections of hundreds of towns, villages, and cities have been brought back to life by restoring their original beauty, charm, and historic integrity. This exciting and constructive movement to preserve the best of yesteryear has been strengthened by planning controls, zoning laws, public financial assistance, and other codes and regulations. There is a growing commitment among property owners not to spoil or destroy the best of all worlds—their home and its environment.

Thousands of owners of antique and historic homes know and appreciate what they have—a rare gem. But an equal number are naive and uninformed. All of these owners are custodians of valuable history. These privileged possessors are in the enviable position of owning something special, unique, and much sought after by ever increasing numbers. However, the one thing an owner of an historic or antique home must do to command and receive Top Dollar from top people is maintain or restore its original character. Thus, don't think twice about asking for professional guidance from historians, architects, and other qualified experts when making any improvements, renovations, or additions. One wrong tap of the hammer might result in a crushing blow to the selling price. For instance, are you the lucky and proud owner of an early 1700s stone house, an 1800s front-to-back, wide-center-hall Colonial, a turn-of-the-century English Tudor, a Georgetown-type townhouse, or one of a dozen other museum pieces? If so, the original owners will come back to haunt you if "someone" has added Formica kitchen cabinets, wall-to-wall carpeting over wide-board floors, suspended block ceilings, floor-to-ceiling ceramic bathrooms, plywood paneling, track lighting, jalousied enclosed porches, plastic shutters, and spackle-painted, exposed hand-hewn beams.

The ultimate achievement of the owner of an historic home is to have that home listed in the *National Register of Historic Places*. An act of Congress, administered by the Department of the Interior's Heritage, Conservation and Recreation Service (HCRS), established the *National Register* to encourage public participation in the preservation of historic properties.

The broad categorization under which homes are eligible for this prestigious designation is that the home, property, or land must have been associated with an historic event or person, have an aesthetic distinction, or be deemed to be of archaeological importance. A section of a community or an entire city block, an important land area, or a portion along a major causeway or waterway are but a few examples of what is known as a district listing in the *National Register of Historic Places*.

Application for this coveted federal recognition involves a reasonable amount of effort by the individual homeowner and much red tape. However, most of this is cost free and well worth the trouble. A home listed in the *National Register* gives the owner a richly deserved sense of pride. Numerous grants for restoring, low-cost interest loans, and various property- and income-tax windfalls are other benefits. A home listed in the *National Register* significantly increases in value.

If you feel your home might be eligible, your first step is to research it and accumulate as much historic data as you can from local libraries, record offices, historic societies, and regional historians. Keep in mind the four general categories of eligibility stated above and the status of your home in relation to them. Have several copies made of the pertinent material. Take a good number of exterior and interior photographs, and don't overlook the importance of old photographs as well.

In every state of the Union and its territories, there is available to you an Historic Preservation Officer or officers. This state official is an integral part of a larger state bureau or division, which may be Conservation, Planning, or Parks. Direct your inquiry by phone, mail, or in person to this office. Your local representative in the State Legislature, your County Clerk, or your Historical Society will promptly help you in making this contact. After contacting him or her, the usual procedure is to complete an application which is then forwarded to the state office. *Do not contact any federal office at this point, as you must start the process at state level.* \*

Upon receipt of your application and other information requested, the State Historic Preservation Officer and his staff may then inspect your home, providing the data submitted qualifies for further interest. After staff recommendation, all material will go before the State Review Board, whose members consist of prominent historians, architects, academics, ecologists, and other experts. Your application, along with the findings of the State Review Board, will then be forwarded to the Heritage Conservation and Recreation Service of the Department of the Interior in Washington, D.C. There, it will be reviewed and acted upon, or a request for additional information might be forthcoming.

The time frame involved from initial contact with the state official to acceptance or rejection of the application by Washington hinges on the speed of the various state- and federal-level departments and the completeness of your portfolio of information. Some final designations have been made in ninety days, but be patient. The wheels of bureaucracy sometimes grind slowly.

Contrary to the common impression of the colossus of government, most home owner applicants have thoroughly enjoyed their relationships with historic-designation officials at both the state and federal levels. These officials are well trained, capable, and helpful, and they sincerely enjoy their work. If for any reason you have difficulty contacting your State Historic Preservation Officer, or you experience unreasonable delays from the state level, write or call:

National Register of Historic Places
U.S. Department of the Interior

---

\*State Historic Preservation Officers may be contacted at the addresses given for all states and the six U.S. territories at the end of this chapter.

Heritage Conservation and Recreation Service (HCRS)
440 G Street N.W.
Washington, D.C. 20243


Before final designation is extended to a homeowner, the local governing body is advised of the government's decision. This is done to alert local officials so that they may properly assess contemplated projects or those already in progress in relationship to an historical-landmark designation.

No legal responsibilities or obligations accompany the historical designation unless the property owner becomes the recipient of any federal, state, and/or local grants or loans for restoration, rehabilitation, or other use. The property owner receiving a loan or grant may be required to maintain the property without substantial alteration for a number of years, depending on the amount of the funds provided. This binding preservation agreement is attached to the property deed. Remember, a homeowner should not begin work or become contractually obligated until the State Historic Preservation Officer and all other loan authorities have approved the project.

The owner of a home listed in the *National Register of Historic Places* is granted special income tax benefits: He or she is permitted to accelerate depreciation on approved restoration or rehabilitation over a period of five years instead of the normal twenty to twenty-five years. This tax write-off is applicable *only* if the property is used or converted to business or rental use (held for the production of income), as defined by the Internal Revenue Service (Sec. 167, Internal Revenue Code of 1954). Therefore, the owner of a designated property used for a personal residence only does not qualify for special benefits under existing federal tax laws, but should check with his or her tax adviser or attorney for any special income- or property-tax benefits under state or local statutes. However, remember that federal or state loans and grants may still be available, regardless of your tax status.

Prior to applying for any loans or grants available to property owners listed in the *National Register,* thoroughly investigate the legal obligations and responsibilities that are mandated. They might include the opening of your home to special public tours; a permanent recorded restriction limiting conversion or major changes in the future without permission; conditions and obligations relating to sale of the property; and income tax effects. Naturally, I feel there is a strong moral obligation upon the owner to maintain and preserve a home listed in the *National Register,* whether legally bound under the loan-grant conditions or basically free by virtue of designation only.

Authorities at both the federal and state level do not take their responsibilities for designation lightly. Sifting, inspecting, and reviewing what is modestly described as voluminous application material is a painstaking and time-consuming task at all levels. Anxious homeowners do become impatient; therefore, I suggest that those who apply do so well in advance of listing their property for sale.

Recognizing that a heavy backlog of applications exists in some areas of our country at the state level, various nonprofit conservation and preservation associations are functioning in an effort to ease the government pressure, preserve the historic property, perform a public service. Once they are aware that a particular home or property has special historic significance, and are reasonably confident of its potential to be listed in the *National Register,* they step in and actually buy the property—if the owner is either very impatient or must sell. Their primary purpose is to preserve an historic place and ensure that it does not fall into the hands of a purchaser who might destroy or mutilate a structure worthy of saving for posterity. This group maintains the property for the interim period required to transfer it to its highest and best historical use.

If you are an anxious seller of what you believe is a home of historical significance, but for any of several reasons your home has not been listed in the *National Register,* determine if any organizations function as described in your area or state. (Due to lack of federal funding and the cost of continuing maintenance, the National Trust for Historic Preservation or the National Park Service rarely acquires property from a homeowner for public use. However, this does not mean that every effort should not be made to investigate acquisition procedures for state- or local-government-funded projects through the State Historic Preservation Officer.) If interested, they will have their own appraisers who are trained and experienced in establishing fair value for *National Register*-type homes. With few exceptions, a home listed in the *National Register,* or one which authorities believe would qualify, usually has a market value far in excess of a comparable home in comparable condition and in a similar location but not qualifying for the *National Register.*

The fact that your home has not been maintained in its original condition or is not in good repair should not be a deterrent for you in making application for *National Register* designation—providing substantial evidence exists that the property meets the basic qualifications. It is also worth noting that a property may qualify under the historical event or person category even though the event or person does not have national significance, if that event or person is historically important in the annals of a state or a local area. In other words, your Uncle George who once slept in your home might prove as historic a local character as George Washington. The emphasis here is on the word *might*. If you reside in a neighborhood or community steeped in special historical significance, do something about it. Appoint yourself a committee of one and start the ball rolling. The tangible and intangible rewards will benefit both you and the members of your community.

All things being equal, if your home has a reasonable chance of qualifying for the *National Register,* delay listing it for sale or remove it from actual listing. Designation increases interest on the part of buyers and investors, which translates to more Top Dollars.

The cumulative list of properties in the *National Register of Historic Places* is published annually, usually on the first Tuesday of February of each year, in what is known as the *Federal Register.* Additions to the *National Register* are published weekly in the *Federal Register.* If you wish to obtain a list of the *National Register of Historic Places,* write to the:

Superintendent of Documents
U.S. Government Printing Office
Washington, D.C. 20402

Ask for Part 2 of the most current edition of the *Federal Register.* It is also likely that you may obtain a copy from your State Historic Preservation Officer. Once you obtain the complete list, you will not find it difficult to locate all the places in your community that are listed in the *National Register.*

### State Historic Preservation Officers

*Alabama:*
Director, Alabama Dept. of Archives and History
Chairman, Alabama Historical Commission
Archives and History Building
Montgomery, AL 36104

*Alaska:*
Chief of History and Archaeology
Division of Parks, Dept. of Natural Resources
619 Warehouse Ave. Suite 210
Anchorage, AK 99501

*American Samoa:*
> Territorial Historic Preservation Officer
> Dept. of Public Works
> Govt. of American Samoa
> Pago Pago, American Samoa 96799

*Arizona:*
> Chief, Natural and Cultural Resource Conservation Section
> Arizona State Parks
> 1688 West Adams
> Phoenix, AZ 85007

*Arkansas:*
> Director, Arkansas Historic Preservation Program
> Suite 500, Continental Bldg.
> Markham and Main Sts.
> Little Rock, AR 72201

*California:*
> Office of Historic Preservation
> California Dept. of Parks and Recreation
> P.O. Box 2390
> Sacramento, CA 95811

*Colorado:*
> State Historic Preservation Officer
> Colorado Heritage Center
> 1300 Broadway
> Denver, CO 80203

*Connecticut:*
> Director, Connecticut Historical Commission
> 59 South Prospect St.
> Hartford, CT 06106

*Delaware:*
> Director, Division of Historical and Cultural Affairs
> Hall of Records
> Dover, DE 19901

*District of Columbia:*
Director, Dept. of Housing and Community Development
1325 G St. N.W.
Washington, D.C. 20005

*Florida:*
Deputy Secretary of State
The Capitol
401 E. Gaines St.
Tallahassee, FL 32304

*Georgia:*
Chief, Historic Preservation Section
Dept. of Natural Resources
270 Washington St. SW
Room 703-C
Atlanta, GA 30334

*Guam:*
Director of Parks and Recreation
Govt. of Guam
P.O. Box 682
Agana, Guam 96910

*Hawaii:*
State Historic Preservation Officer
Dept. of Land and Natural Resources
P.O. Box 621
Honolulu, HI 96809

*Idaho:*
Historic Preservation Coordinator
Idaho Historical Society
610 North Julia Davis Dr.
Boise, ID 83706

*Illinois:*
Director, Dept. of Conservation
602 State Office Bldg.

400 So. Spring St.
Springfield, IL 62706

*Indiana:*

Director, Dept. of Natural Resources
608 State Office Bldg.
Indianapolis, IN 46204

*Iowa:*

Director, Iowa State Historical Dept.
Division of Historic Preservation
26 E. Market St.
Iowa City, IA 52240

*Kansas:*

Executive Director, Kansas State Historical Society
120 W. 10th St.
Topeka, KS 66612

*Kentucky:*

Director, Kentucky Heritage Commission
104 Bridge St.
Frankfort, KY 40601

*Louisiana:*

Asst. Secretary, Office of Program Development
P.O. Box 44247
Baton Rouge, LA 70804

*Maine:*

Director, Maine Historic Preservation Commission
31 Western Ave.
Augusta, ME 04330

*Maryland:*

State Historic Preservation Officer
John Shaw House
21 State Circle
Annapolis, MD 21401

*Massachusetts:*
Executive Director, Massachusetts Historical Commission
294 Washington St.
Boston, MA 02108

*Michigan:*
Director, Michigan History Division
Dept. of State
Lansing, MI 48918

*Minnesota:*
Director, Minnesota Historical Society
690 Cedar St.
St. Paul, MN 55101

*Mississippi:*
Director, State of Mississippi
Dept. of Archives and History
P.O. Box 571
Jackson, MS 39205

*Missouri:*
State Historic Preservation Officer
State Dept. of Natural Resources
P.O. Box 176
Jefferson City, MO 65101

*Montana:*
Director, Montana Historical Society
225 No. Roberts St.
Veterans Memorial Bldg.
Helena, MT 59601

*Nebraska:*
Director, The Nebraska State Historical Society
1500 R Street
Lincoln, NE 68508

*Nevada*
State Historical Preservation Officer

Division of Historic Preservation and Archaeology
Capitol Complex
Carson City, NV 89710

*New Hampshire:*
Commissioner, Dept. of Resources and Economic
Development
P.O. Box 846
Concord, NH 03301

*New Jersey:*
Commissioner, Dept. of Environmental Protection
P.O. Box 1420
Trenton, NJ 08625

*New Mexico:*
State Historic Preservation Officer
New Mexico Historic Preservation Program
Dept. of Education, Finance and Cultural Affairs
c/o New Mexico State Library
P.O. Box 1629
Santa Fe, NM 87503

*New York:*
Commissioner, Parks and Recreation
Agency Bldg. No. 1
Empire State Plaza
Albany, NY 12238

*North Carolina:*
Director, Division of Archives and History
Dept. of Cultural Resources
109 E. Jones St.
Raleigh, NC 27611

*North Dakota:*
Superintendent, State Historical Society of North Dakota
Liberty Memorial Bldg.
Bismark, ND 58501

*North Mariana Islands:*
Historic Preservation Officer
c/o Dept. of Community and Cultural Affairs
Commonwealth of Northern Mariana Islands
Saipan, Mariana Islands 96950

*Ohio:*
Director, The Ohio Historical Society
Interstate 71 at 17th Ave.
Columbus, OH 43211

*Oklahoma:*
State Historic Preservation Officer
235 Pasteur Bldg.
1111 North Lee
Oklahoma City, OK 73103

*Oregon:*
State Parks Superintendent
525 Trade St. S.E.
Salem, OR 97310

*Pennsylvania:*
Pennsylvania Historical and Museum Commission
P.O. Box 1026
Harrisburg, PA 17120

*Commonwealth of Puerto Rico:*
Institute of Puerto Rico Culture
Apartado 4184
San Juan, PR 00905

*Rhode Island:*
Director, Rhode Island Dept. of Community Affairs
150 Washington St.
Providence, RI 02903

*South Carolina:*
Director, State Archives Dept.
1430 Senate St.

Columbia, SC 29211

*South Dakota:*
State Historical Preservation Officer
Historical Preservation Center
Univ. of South Dakota
Alumni House
Vermillion, SD 57069

*Tennessee:*
Executive Director, Tennessee Historical Commission
170 2nd Avenue N., Suite 100
Nashville, TN 37219

*Texas:*
Executive Director, Texas State Historical Commission
P.O. Box 12276
Capital Station
Austin, TX 78711

*Trust Territory of the Pacific Islands:*
Historic Preservation Officer,
Land Resources Branch
Dept. of Resources and Development, TTPI
Saipan, Mariana Islands 96950

*Utah:*
Executive Director, Dept. of Development Services
Room 104
State Capitol
Salt Lake City, UT 84114

*Vermont:*
Director, Vermont Division for Historic Preservation
Pavilion Office Bldg.
Montpelier, VT 05602

*Virginia:*
Virginia Historic Landmarks Commission
221 Governor St.

Richmond, VA 23219

*Virgin Islands:*
Planning Director, Virgin Islands Planning Board
Charlotte Amalie
St. Thomas, VI 00801

*Washington:*
State Historic Preservation Officer
111 W. 21st Ave.
KL-11
Olympia, WA 98504

*West Virginia:*
State Historic Preservation Officer
Historic Preservation Unit, Dept. of Culture and History
State Capitol Complex
Charleston, WV 25305

*Wisconsin:*
Director, State Historical Society of Wisconsin
816 State St.
Madison, WI 53706

*Wyoming:*
Director: Wyoming Recreation Commission
604 E. 25th St.
Box 309
Cheyenne, WY 82001

*National Trust for Historic Preservation:*
President, National Trust for Historic Preservation
740 Jackson Pl. N.W.
Washington, D.C. 20006

# 15

## *Togetherness: Cooperatives (Co-ops) and Condominiums*

Home to great numbers of our population—the no-lawn-mower elite— is a cooperative or condominium. In major cities throughout the country and in resort areas of the western and Sun Belt States, this form of home ownership has experienced tremendous popularity and growth. In many ways it is much easier to sell a co-op or condo for Top Dollar than it is to sell the conventional single-family home. If you are planning to sell your cooperative or condominium, the following special guidelines might prove helpful.

### Condominium Sellers

- Prepare an accurate floor plan showing ceiling heights and number and size of closets and windows in all rooms.
- Obtain several copies of the original offering brochure of the building, if available. This should include information pertaining to the special extras offered, such as swimming pools, meeting rooms, tennis courts, various services, and shopping facilities.
- Prepare several copies of a schedule listing all current costs

—except mortgage financing—such as monthly maintenance, utilities, taxes, insurance, parking or garages (if provided), and any other routine or normal services.

- Obtain current information from primary banking institutions as to the status of mortgage financing presently available.
- Request from the management office or other appropriate source the sale price of the last ten units sold in the building. Try to obtain similar information on units sold in other buildings in the vicinity. Investigate what new condominiums are selling for—either those under construction or those recently completed. The information will provide a basis for your asking price.
- Prepare a schedule comparing general maintenance costs over the last three years; do not include mortgage financing.
- Try to obtain at least five letters of recommendation about the complex from other owners in the building.
- Prepare a list of all pertinent information that might be of interest to a purchaser, such as schools, medical facilities, public transportation, churches and synagogues, child-care facilities, and climate and recreation in the area. Also, prepare a general statement of the age, status, and interests of those occupying units in the building, *i.e.,* professionals, retirees, singles, *etc.*
- Prepare a list of background information on all owners of units on your floor and those immediately above and below.
- Obtain a statement from management, signed by a principal authority, setting forth the general and overall physical condition of the entire building and all facilities.

It is advised that you combine all the information, with the exception of recent sales and pricing of comparable units, setting forth the above in an attractive package or brochure to be made available to both brokers and potential purchasers of your condominium unit. If possible, have at least thirty-five copies made.

Many condominiums have been successfully sold by the owner through small advertisements in major newspapers which publish throughout the country. The brochure outlined above might bring especially good results if you are advertising on your own, but you should also prepare it if you are selling through a regional broker.

Marketing of your condominium should not be limited to the firm managing the building, as is often the case, but, if it is not contrary to any legal obligation, should also be given to many active brokers in the are who specialize in the sale of condo units. If you believe that your area attracts vacationers or retirees, list the sale with national brokerage firms throughout the country on an open-listing basis.

Determine by survey or investigation the type of purchaser most likely to be interested in your building. Once you have made that judgment, prepare your condominium unit in such a way as to make it as attractive as possible to that most likely purchaser.

Do not hesitate to make as many cosmetic improvements as necessary to make your unit more attractive. If common hallways need perking up and management is reluctant to respond, discuss with other occupants a joint improvement effort.

An effective selling tool has been to offer units fully or partially furnished as part of the asking price. This is particularly true in parts of the country where condominiums are selling to out-of-state buyers, as the cost of moving household furniture from one part of the country to another may be more than what the buyers' furniture is worth.

## Cooperative Sellers

The primary concerns of those wishing to purchase cooperatives are:

- Monthly maintenance cost and the portion that is tax deductible
- The financial position of the corporation owning the building as to present debt and anticipated refinancing or borrowing needs
- Overall physical condition of the building and what, if any, major expenditures are anticipated
- Services available, such as security, elevator operators, doormen, delivery, *etc.*
- Any proposed changes in the immediate neighborhood which would have a positive or negative effect on life-style and values
- Type of occupants, with special emphasis on life-style, age, average income, profession, or occupation
- Views, light, and physical condition of the individual co-op apartment
- Maintenance costs over the last three years and projected costs for the next three years
- Selling price of apartments within the complex during the past three years, with emphasis on those sold in the last twelve months
- Bylaws of the corporation and attitudes of the co-op board regarding percentage of financing permitted for purchase, pets, children, certain occupations, life-styles, net worth, and income.

Be prepared to have all of the above information readily available to the real estate professionals and purchasers, along with a detailed floor plan. Management of the larger cooperatives is usually in the hands of major firms who maintain separate brokerage divisions for selling them. If you consider granting an exclusive right to sell to the management firm of your co-op, limit the period to thirty days if possible. If the firm is not successful during that period, list your apartment with at least ten major brokerage firms specializing in the sale of cooperative apartments.

If your co-op is located in an area that has been attracting foreign purchasers, give consideration to advertising its availability in several of the major overseas newspapers, through brokers or on your own—providing you have listed your co-op on an open-listing arrangement.

Do not hesitate to update your unit with improvements—air conditioning in needed areas, new kitchen and bathroom fixtures, or any other expenditures necessary to make the home more attractive. Most purchasers today neither have the time nor wish to make the effort to physically improve the co-op after purchase, but they are most willing to pay Top Dollar for one in move-in condition.

Finally, investigate thoroughly all available avenues of cooperative financing and have the information ready for prospective purchasers.

An owner of a condominium or cooperative apartment should be prepared to close within thirty days if a purchaser so desires. Not being able to do so has proved a major stumbling block to Top Dollar sales of these types of units. Condo and co-op purchasers seem to want to occupy "yesterday" once they have an approved commitment for financing and other requirements, in contrast with conventional-home purchasers, who are normally more flexible.

Make whatever arrangements are necessary to have your apartment available for inspection throughout the day and early evening hours. Most brokers, particularly in larger cities, have difficulty gaining access to the owner's apartment at all times. Establish some procedure with the superintendent or doorman whereby listing brokers may gain entry when you or members of your household are not at home. Purchasers are as unpredictable as hurricanes. If selling is your goal, you will just have to put up with the idiosyncrasies of the process and the people.

Once you have established your Top Dollar asking price and have made every effort to justify that price by rising above most of the competition, be firm and stick to it for at least the first sixty days of showing.

Cooperative apartment owners should become personally familiar with all members of the administrative board in an effort to determine their individual and joint attitudes toward the interpretation of the bylaws and other policies in admitting new purchasers. This should be done prior to the listing of the apartment. These policies should be firmly conveyed to all listing brokers so their screening process is done in accordance with these policies.

Even those who live in condominiums are subject to some review of their prospective buyer, no matter how subtle. In other words, the other owners within the building may not actually vote to accept the new buyer, but the fine print in your contract usually grants them first refusal of a prospective buyer of your condominium, and the threat of this alone may squelch your deal. Such was the case when former President Richard Nixon decided to move back to New York City and, after failing admittance to either a cooperative or condominium, finally resorted to buying a townhouse of his own.

All indications point to continued strong demand for condominiums and cooperatives. Smaller families, the high divorce rate, and lawn mowers that don't start are but a few of the reasons your cooperative or condominium will be a much sought-after home by the purchaser of tomorrow. Today's owners who wish to sell will likely be in an enviable position as costs continue to mount for new building construction—and also because many of the co-op and condo units built ten or fifteen years ago provide more space and charm than those of today.

# 16
## *Taming the White Elephant*

So you fear you have a white elephant on your hands. Or perhaps someone, maybe even your broker, has told you so. Well, let me say, it ain't necessarily so. For never have I come across a home that, with a little thought and imagination, couldn't be made saleable. Indeed, whenever this happens, I am reminded of the old cliche, if you've got a lemon, make lemonade.

Take, for instance, that imposing 12-, 16- or 20-room Victorian home standing so majestically along Main Street, U.S.A. Why, a few years ago, when families were larger and the upkeep of such a place was lower, it might have even been considered an "easy sell." But today, despite the fact that it might be structurally sound and in beautiful condition—it might even have a fresh coat of paint—no one seems interested in it. That's because it has little, if any, insulation (not even a storm window!), and it costs $4,000 a year to heat. This, you might say, is a white elephant...but not if you look at it in other than a traditional sense, as something other than a single-family home.

That's right, take a minute and sit down to list *all* the possibilities for that home: It could be converted into a boarding house, a retirement home, or an apartment complex. It could be a small private school or a day-care center. It could become an antique shop, a boutique, an art gallery, a restaurant, or a medical arts center. Or maybe a small corporate office, a cottage industry, a mail-order firm, an advertising agency, a research center or laboratory, an upholstery shop, an architect's or lawyer's office or, yes, even a real estate office. In other words, it could be anything *but* a white elephant.

In fact, with prime commercial space going for more than $20 a square foot, your home has become most attractive to many of these professionals who, in addition to seeking a bargain, will jump at any chance to work within a residential setting. Now, all you must do is check your local zoning regulations, and then, if there are restrictions to non-residential use of that home, be prepared to go to your local planning board and ask for a variance. Again it has been my experience that the people who sit on these committees—in many cases, your very best friend or neighbor—actually welcome the possibility of a new resident who will provide the community with a service and will do so without increasing traffic or noise levels and without changing the exterior of the home. Sometimes these planners even see the change as an enhancement of *their* property values. Even if they don't, if your proposal is rejected, you can always appeal the decision in a higher court, but be sure to take along an experienced attorney, one who may even volunteer his or her services on a contingency basis or for a percentage of the eventual sale, if approved.

Now, that takes care of the so-called white elephant that is in good condition, but what about the one that is not; the one with inadequate wiring, leaky plumbing, a collapsing portico, and a kitchen that looks custom-made for Wilma Flintstone! You guess it would take about $60,000 to resurrect the place. What now?

Well, you could always throw it on the market at a disgustingly low price and unload it. Or you could try for Top Dollar. You could offer it at a fairly reasonable price—as a "Handyman Special"—to a young contractor, thus giving him and his family a place to live for a minimum down payment and low monthly payments while he restores the house for you. Sure, make him a partner and tell him you'll split the material costs if he donates the labor to make the repairs. Then, when the house is sold, presumably now for Top Dollar, you can either split the profit or work out some percentage figure of that excess amount. Arrangements such as this have worked; I've seen it happen, but I've also seen that it takes some thought…and some patience.

On the other hand, maybe you're offering a baby white elephant, a house that is too *small.* Maybe it's a trailer home or a garage that's been converted into a home. In this case, check first with your neighbors to see if either of them would be interested in buying it, for whatever reason, or, if not, if they would sell you a portion of their adjoining land. Sometimes only a few more feet on each side of your narrow property will make it appear larger. Then, too, make the house itself appear larger: Add a front porch, attach a carport, or erect some trellis to give the effect of another wing to the house. And turn it into a real dollhouse: Attach shutters and windowboxes to the few windows, stick a few feet of picket fence into the ground, and plant a row of zinnias; anything to attract the one-in-a-million buyer who actually wants a mini-home. Once more, I have seen this work.

Then, what about the rather manageable home that is in fairly good condition but no longer in a prime residential location…the home that was once in an all-American Norman Rockwell-type neighborhood but now, for one reason or another, is not. What can be done with this potential white elephant?

Again you must explore what other possibilities that house may have as something other than another single-family home.

And again you must check to see if present zoning regulations will permit such a use, or if you can obtain a variance. Then you must determine what it would cost to make the necessary conversion into multiple residence, part residence/part commercial, or all commercial property—it may be nothing more than adding a skylight to a second-story bedroom and thus attracting an architect or an artist—and if the expense, time, and effort it would take to do so would be worth the price you could then get for your home.

Here your local brokers, bankers, and contractors can be most helpful. They can tell you the *true* trend of your neighborhood, and they can tell you what completed projects such as the one you have in mind have brought in dollars and cents. Furthermore, they can tell you what federal, urban renewal, or community action funding may be available to you, or what loans may be granted using a signed contract or long-term lease as collateral. They may even tell you whether to commission architectural drawings or models and to collect several builders' bids to show a prospective buyer and let *him* make the conversion. Or they may tell you whether to proceed with the alterations yourself, then lease it out as an income-producing property.

For example, at one time a client of mine wanted to sell his large Colonial home. But because it was located directly across from the entrance to the emergency ward of the only hospital in the county, with all those ambulances zooming in and out at all hours of the day and night, he could barely get $12,000 for it. Then, when I suggested we approach several of the physicians who regularly treat patients at the hospital, asking them if they would like an office right across the street, he took me up on the idea—and today he has an annual rental income in excess of $100,000!

In other cases, though, you may discover, as a result of your investigation, that the land your house sits on is more valuable as a parking lot, or whatever, than the home itself. Then you may want to determine what it would cost to move that house—actually it's neither easy nor inexpensive—and sell the land. However, I know one family who sold their lot to a fast-food chain and, as a result, had more than enough money to move their modest home to a brand-new half-acre building site a few miles away *and* to totally redecorate it! But the decision is up to you. You are the one who must do the homework and collect all the information necessary to reduce the risk factor of such a decision to the absolute minimum.

But what do you do, you ask, if you *know* you not only have a white elephant but one with one foot in the grave? For instance, your home has incurred extensive fire or flood damage, or, because of years of benign neglect, it has gone past the point of no return. What now?

Well, whether or not you've been able to collect from the insurance company for your losses, you can still salvage a little more out of your house. You can sell the moldings, the fireplace mantels, parquet flooring, copper pipes, even the hardware, the light switches, and the doorknobs, if not the doors themselves. And then you can sell the land. In some cases, though, you may want to take the extra effort (and expense) to bring a bulldozer in to level whatever is left on that property, for many times, if a prospective buyer can see your lot as a ready-to-go building site, you can get more money for it. Remember, especially in the event you do own a real-life white elephant, getting Top Dollar isn't necessarily getting the highest price; it may be nothing more than *getting the most money under the present conditions.*

Remember, too, that in the case of the real or supposed white elephant, beauty is truly in the eye of the beholder. Indeed, what may seem to you to be a supreme headache might, to someone else, be an incredible joy. That's right, when selling this unique kind of home, you need always keep in mind that now, more than ever, you are looking for a unique buyer. You are not marketing your home, through promotion or advertising, to the run-of-the-mill home-buying public. You will need to gear your sales pitch to that special customer and then sit back and be patient. More than likely, within time, someone will come along who's been trekking through the jungles of your community just looking for a "white elephant."

Speaking of jungles, I once was involved in the sale of a home that appeared to be situated right in the midst of one. Located some 2,500 feet off the main road, this property had been vacant just long enough to become totally overgrown with ivy and sumac. Thus, the little two-bedroom cottage was camouflaged to the point that anyone passing by would figure that the only thing that could survive in that jungle would be a white elephant.

Well, for a minimum of investment, I hired six young college students, all home for Easter vacation, to clear away the ivy, cut down the dead trees (which were then sold for firewood), bulldoze the stumps and regrade the driveway, cover it with fresh gravel—and totally clean the house from cellar to attic. Then, after we let a little sunlight filter in, I placed the property on the market and sold it before school recessed again for the summer. And the absentee owners, who had expected a forced sale somewhere in the neighborhood of $20,000, were surprised —and overjoyed—when I brought them a buyer at $45,000. But even that wasn't all that difficult. All I did was wait for a prospect who had turned thumbs down on every other property for not being private enough!

Indeed, there is a master out there for any white elephant you might run across.

# 17
## *Should You Break It Up?*

Those of you who own a home or estate involving more than a normal-size lot might want to consider selling less than all the property involved. I am frequently asked by those anticipating the sale of their home if they should include all the acreage, the guest house, and two extra building lots adjoining the primary property, or the parcel on the other side of the road. What they are really asking is: "Will I get more money breaking it up, or selling it as one piece?"

In the majority of cases, I have found the owner was basically interested in selling the main residence. There was no objection to holding the adjoining lots, land, or guest house, providing this strategy would eventually result in a quick sale of the main residence without substantially reducing the price. This scenario is usually accompanied by the story of how the neighbor who had a home and forty acres on the market for $140,000 for over a year with few offers, decided to offer the home for sale with only five acres for $95,000, and it was snapped up within a week. Now he has the thirty-five remaining acres on the market for $55,000, and a dozen people are interested.

However, don't make the mistake I heard about while lecturing on the West Coast recently. There, a man who owned a lovely older home on eight acres of land wanted to build a smaller retirement home on the same property and offer for sale the original home and four acres. Well, fine. . . but he was warned: Don't build until the main house and four acres are sold. Turning a deaf ear, though, he built the smaller home, and, worse yet, he built it only 400 feet from the main house. When asked why, he merely replied, "Well, I wanted to use the same well and septic and power line." That was four years ago. Today the man and his wife still live in the older home and, finally, with no buyer for either in sight, have decided to rent the smaller one.

On the other hand, sub-dividing can work. Using the example of the neighbor who owned forty acres, let me explain a few of the reasons why:

- Many more buyers are looking in the price range of under $100,000 than over $100,000, thereby swelling the ranks of potential homeowners investigating the $95,000 sale in contrast to the $140,000 offering.

- Those interested in buying just some acreage are not usually willing to purchase a home. So, when the thirty-five acres become available, a good number of buyers were attracted.

- As a rule, lending institutions evaluating properties for mortgages give greater consideration to the value of the residence than to the adjoining land. They do not appraise the land as individual, saleable units, but as an enhancement value to the primary property. This procedure enables a prospective purchaser of the home with only five acres to obtain excellent financing—a basic stimulant to the buyer. But those wishing to buy the $140,000 parcel might be unable to obtain sufficient financing, even though they are desirous of buying the home with all forty acres.

- Prospective purchasers may pay Top Dollar for the home with five acres, providing they are given the right of first refusal to buy the additional acreage at the same price offered for sale, when and if the seller decides to sell. There are those buyers who are even more likely to make this move if the seller will warrant by agreement that the adjoining acreage will be restricted to residential purposes or a minimum of only a few homes.

There are exceptions and there are exceptions. Not every home with some acreage or extra buildings necessarily follows the above pattern. Nor should one conclude that breaking it up is always the answer. Variables include price range, location, neighborhood, access to the retained property, income tax ramifications, and overall goals of the seller.

Part of the process in determining the asking price of the property, as outlined in Chapter 2, "What Is Top Dollar?", is to be advised whether the "all" (sale in one piece) is or is not the sum of the parts.

If the main dwelling is in a special category, possessing unusual architectural integrity, great size, or special use, it may preclude a sale without the proper acreage and other amenities necessary to its distinctive nature. Many cases can be cited where, had the owner sold part of the land prior to sale of the main home, the home itself would have been marketable only at a drastic price reduction. Homeowners should *never* sell any part of property adjoining the primary residence prior to selling the residence itself. Doing so involves a major risk and potential loss, and could also have far-flung negative income tax ramifications under current IRS tax laws. (See Chapter 12, "Avoiding the Income Tax Bite.")

Property with a reasonable amount of acreage but a minimum amount of road frontage does not lend itself well to the breaking up process. It leaves the main residence vulnerable to disturbing problems of entrance and exit to the adjoining parcel. Most buyers are very sensitive to this environmental negative.

There is still, at present, a desire among buyers to obtain as much land as possible with the primary home. However, as real estate taxes continue to skyrocket, the demand for acreage surrounding a primary home is diminishing. Even affluent purchasers must compromise to make their single-home ownership economically feasible. If this trend of ever-increasing prices relating to home ownership continues (and every indication points in that direction), sellers of larger-than-average parcels of land will be compelled to break them up in order to fulfill the Great American Dream of home ownership.

Exceptions today are frequently noted in the sale of luxury homes and estates, as the market continues strong for the $500,000 to $1 million category. Real estate professionals agree it is sometimes easier in today's market to sell a $500,000 home or estate than one in the $150,000 to $250,000 price range. On the other end of the scale, if the present market value of your property is in the $40,000 to $60,000 range, it will probably sell just as fast without that extra acre or two.

Throughout the country, it is becoming increasingly difficult to obtain a minor subdivision approval from local zoning or planning boards for sale of smaller parcels. Be sure to check with local authorities as to the procedures and necessary requirements before making any representations or decisions about subdividing your property. This will ensure that you are in compliance with present statutes and regulations. Also be aware that state and local laws are now requiring various surveys and engineering data to be provided by the owner before granting permission to subdivide or sell subdivided parcels or lots.

# IV

# *Making the Best of the Worst of Times*

# 18

## *Dealing with Not-So-Silent Partners*

Mother passed away more than a year ago, leaving her modest village home to her three daughters who were all married and scattered across the country. They were to meet with me a couple of days after the funeral, however, in order to discuss a listing price for the home. But when I arrived in the midst of a tug-of-war, not only over the antique armoire in the bedroom, but also the pressed-glass flower bowl on the dining table, I soon realized that attempting to come to any consensus at this time would be futile.

And I was right. After being asked what I thought the place was worth, and answering with a figure somewhere around $85,000 based on current market value, the eldest daughter, who had not been around for twenty years, cried, "Oh, that's too high. We'll *never* sell it for that."

Yet the youngest daughter, who had married a local contractor, thought the suggested price was too low. "My husband says it would cost at least twice that to build the house today, and we shouldn't take a nickel less than $150,000 for it," she exclaimed.

And to make matters worse, the middle child, the one who had obviously made the best marriage, off-handedly remarked, "Oh, it doesn't really make any difference whether it's $10,000 one way or another; the main thing is to sell the house."

I agreed with her second thought, but I also knew that in their present frame of mind none of them would change their initial opinion for some time. And they didn't. So we didn't even list the house for another six months, and then, because it had stood empty and because vandalism had occurred, they finally had to accept an offer about $12,000 *less* than my original estimate. In hindsight, all they had to do was agree to hire an appraiser, or obtain a consensus of appraisals, and get on with it. But they didn't.

The negative aspects of human nature are nothing new. They've existed since Eve joined Adam, although it seems, in the world of real estate transactions anyway, they're surfacing with increasing regularity. And yet, even under the most strained of circumstances surrounding a death, divorce, or shattered partnership, there are some guidelines to be followed if you hope to get Top Dollar for the property in question.

The first basic step to be taken in an effort to avoid endless delays, property deterioration, and loss of money in an estate disposition, divorce proceedings, or joint ownership conflict is to obtain expert professional guidance in determining the highest and best use and value. In Chapter 2, "What Is Top Dollar?", these procedures are outlined in detail. Personal animosity, bitterness, and greed injected into the determination will accomplish only one thing—the property will sell for far less than it should under reasonable conditions with reasonable care.

Many case histories show that the general public soon becomes aware of the internal strife, with potential purchasers taking one of two positions: Either they do not wish to become involved and won't touch the offering with a ten-foot pole, or they feel they can take advantage of the situation and eventually pick it up for a song. It may be a worn-out cliché, but it is appropriate to these conditions—don't wash your dirty linen in public.

## Estates

For those of you who may become involved in an estate settlement where the primary home is part of the estate, may I suggest the following course of action. If you genuinely feel that the selling price determined for the estate is unsatisfactory, or a difference of opinion exists among the heirs, agree to retain a professional appraiser satisfactory to all those in disagreement. Let the appraiser representing each member of the estate choose another appraiser, with the understanding that their joint decision be final and acceptable to all involved. For example, if there are three heirs to one estate—two who are in agreement and one who is not—the two who agree pick one appraiser; the third selects his or her own. The two appraisers make their individual investigations and retain a third qualified appraiser. The final decision of the three is the determined fixed price. It is possible that the three professionals will have areas of disagreement, but usually the difference is not substantial. The cost involved may either be charged to the estate or, by agreement, be the independent responsibility of each heir. The price is usually nominal and well worth the resulting peace in the family.

It is not uncommon for each beneficiary to be represented individually by his or her own attorney once the sparks begin to fly in estate disputes. If you feel more comfortable with your own attorney representing you, rather than having one lawyer for the entire estate, that's fine. But don't argue with him—follow his sage advice. The majority of problems arising from estate disagreements between the recipients do not usually stem from the home to be sold itself, but from the disposition of other assets, oral promises made during the life of the deceased, absence of a good will or no will at all, or past ill feelings now surfacing. The battering ram for all of this is a good home that should be sold at a good price.

Your position or the position of others involved may be well founded. But don't take it out on the poor house! Determine the best price possible under existing market conditions and *sell it* as quickly as possible. Place the funds received from the sale in an estate or escrow account with an attorney. If you must argue about who gets what, then do so with the help of your attorney and the courts. From the point of view of a real estate professional, this is the best advice I can give you.

It is wise to have a member of the family or a representative of the estate be readily available to real estate agents during the period when the home is shown. The property should be well maintained, and all charges for taxes, insurance, and utilities should be paid promptly. This will avoid any real or psychological negatives which might occur to haunt the sale. Property values of an estate home quickly diminish if public notices appear for nonpayment of taxes, judgments are issued for routine unpaid bills, and notice of building code or zoning violations are circulated in the community. This frequently occurs, particularly when the heirs involved reside out of the area. Local bank loans are readily available to estates for meeting current obligations during the selling period in the event estate funds are frozen or nonexistent, or individual heirs do not wish to cover these costs until the sale is made.

In addition to the agreed selling price, all those involved in the sale should agree as to the method of listing, the commission to be paid, the occupancy date, the personal property to be included, and whether the estate will consider financing, such as a mortgage to the purchaser. A memorandum "agreeing to agree" should be prepared by the estate attorney and executed by all those involved.

## Separation and Divorce

With the divorce rate touching nearly 50 percent of American couples, thousands of homes must be sold annually as part of separation or divorce agreements. The home becomes an emotional as well as an economic base for divorce settlement proceedings. It is difficult to separate these two factors, but we must, if the home is to be sold at the best price in the market place.

The most common problem in a marital breakup is that the primary home gets pushed from pillar to post and used as leverage by either party to reach an agreement concerning child support, division of other assets, amount of alimony, and who is going to live where and for how long. If the home must be sold, the two people and their respective attorneys should immediately determine the marketing procedure without a public airing of their problems. The home should be well maintained and occupied, if possible, and every effort should be made to avoid the usual signs of depression and despair that are normal under these difficult circumstances.

Marketing procedures in a divorce situation are generally comparable to other house-selling situations highlighted throughout this book. The major differences are the inability of the estranged couple and their respective attorneys to agree on establishing the asking price, and determining distribution of the funds from the eventual sale.

One easy solution is for the couple to allow their individual attorneys each to select a qualified appraiser to evaluate the property and then have these two appraisers appoint a third. The determination of the three appraisers should be final and agreed to by both parties. The second hurdle can be overcome by placing monies received from the sale of the house in a joint escrow account, with both attorneys involved, until mutual agreement is reached as to division of the funds. In the event an agreement becomes impossible, the courts must decide as to the allocation.

What does all this accomplish?—the primary objective, which is the sale of the home at Top Dollar with the minimum delay and deterioration. With the actual funds in hand, the couple is now a major step closer to resolving the final details of the divorce. Monies are now available to them for meeting current obligations such as school and college expenses for children, personal needs, and attorney's fees. The heavy costs of carrying the home's mortgage payments, taxes, and other related charges cease, relieving some pressures and clearing the way for more amicable and reasonable negotiations.

In the event both parties are physically removed from the area during the period from the initial separation to the final sale of the home, consideration should be given to obtaining a housesitter-type of tenant on a month-to-month basis. This is important for security and general maintenance reasons, as well as for showing the home to prospective buyers. Abandonment of a home under *any* conditions usually reduces the value and marketability by 20 to 30 percent or more within a short time.

If economic conditions are not favorable at the time the home must be sold, consider an interim rental at a rate sufficient to cover the carrying costs. Attorneys often suggest that the husband buy the home from the wife, or vice versa, at the appraised price or even less, with a written understanding to this effect: If the house is sold within one year following the transaction for an amount in excess of the selling price agreed upon by the couple, the amount of surplus will be divided between the two. This delaying action has proven to be successful in many cases, as it provides a home for either party and achieves independence, with both parties sharing directly and indirectly in the benefits.

Most attorneys involved in divorce actions demonstrate a sincere and sensitive attitude toward disposition of the home involved. They know all of the practical alternatives to follow so that the primary home will be sold without delay at the price it should bring.

## Joint Ownership

Whether they are related or not, when two or more people acquire a partnership home or joint ownership, it is often the beginning of the end. One factor contributing to this may be the lack of formal agreement. This is a legal instrument prepared by an attorney and setting forth the rights, responsibilities, and options of each joint owner.

On the day of closing, a mutual understanding, in writing, should outline procedures to follow in the event of death, illness, financial collapse, disenchantment, change of life-style or residence, infrequency of occupancy, improvements to be made, sharing of expense, evaluation of offers to sell or buy adjoining parcels, and dozens of additional potential battlegrounds.

Partnerships that cannot be dissolved amicably often become one of the thousands of court cases eventually resulting in a public auction or a partition sale. The latter is a legal remedy available in many states, wherein one of the owners forces a public sale of the property when mutual agreement as to selling price, *etc.* is impossible to reach. Published legal notices pertaining to the distribution of property and the assumed knowledge on the part of the general public of the internal friction usually result in the property being sold for much less than normal market conditions.

Though each of the parties involved believes he can justify his individual position, this does not solve the problem. Arbitration by experienced and impartial professional arbitrators can. If the aggrieved partners turn to them to solve their differences, the property involved will eventually bring a much higher price, save a great deal of embarrassment for all concerned, and substantially reduce the cost of the experience of joint ownership.

# 19

## *How to Survive a Company Transfer*

Recently I had a client who thought he had an unsolvable problem. His boss had just informed him that, within sixty days, he was to be made a district manager, but in a district half way across the country. And when I told him it would take a real estate wizard, plus an incredible amount of luck, to move his three-bedroom ranch that quickly, he said he couldn't see any alternative to trying. After all, he knew he didn't want to leave his wife and children behind for any period of time, and he certainly didn't want to leave the house vacant either. That's when I suggested, "Maybe your boss will buy it."

He asked, and, lo and behold! his problem was solved. For, luckily enough, this man worked for one of the more than one thousand firms that, because they frequently transfer employees to various company locations, also provide an on-the-spot home-buying service to make that move as simple as possible.

In fact, starting in the late 1960s, as companies expanded into nationwide branch locations, so did the problems of coping with the transferred employees' families and homes. Many employers agreed to buy their homes at current market value, to pay the moving costs, and to assume the burden of finding new homes for the uprooted families. As the activity increased, so did the firms' investment in purchasing the homes and the headaches of coping with resale arrangements and interim property management.

Recognizing this national problem, American ingenuity came to the rescue with the establishment of several firms specializing in a full home-buying and relocation service—providing the aspirin that cured the headache. The basic concept is this: The employing firm enters into a contract with the relocation service, which then assumes full responsibility for purchasing the transferred employee's home and makes all arrangements for the physical move to the new location. Additionally, a new home is found for the employee; financing, if needed, is arranged; and everything possible is done to smooth the transition.

This valuable fringe benefit relieves the employee of the home-selling process; eliminates the burden of owning two homes simultaneously, perhaps in different parts of the country; and reduces pressure and tension in the moving family. In addition, where an entire firm relocates as a unit, the relocation service undertakes the responsibility of buying all the homes and moving all the employees in a one-shot deal. Contracts providing employers with a full-service relocation program vary to some extent in the services offered and the fees charged, but the basic concepts are similar.

An employer must have a contractual arrangement with the home-buying service for an employee to be eligible for the benefits of these services. Thousands of homeowners have availed themselves of quick sales of their homes by this method over the past ten years. It is obviously filling a need for both employers and employees, as witnessed by the success and growth of the major relocation companies.

If you are a homeowner and have been advised by your firm that you are being transferred, investigate the home-buying/

relocation method of selling. I suggest the following:

- Determine from your employer the name of the relocation firm serving the company. If your employer does not provide this service and advises you that the move is entirely up to you, suggest to your company's officials the possibility of investigating such a program, as they might not be aware of its existence.
- If eligible, your firm will put you in contact with the relocation representative, who will outline the procedure. You will be advised to obtain a market-value appraisal of your home from the local real estate professionals or firms on their approved list.
- Once the appraisal is completed, you will be advised by the relocation company of the price offered for your home. This is a guaranteed cash offer usually available for sixty to ninety days, depending upon the basic contract provisions with your company. *You do not have to accept this offer until the time expires.* Without endangering the offer in any way, you may take whatever steps you deem necessary to sell your home for more than what was offered.
- If you sincerely believe the offer submitted is not fair, notify the relocation home-buying service, state your case, and ask for a review.
- Do not be disillusioned if, through your own selling efforts, you receive offers of a few thousand dollars in excess of the company's, as you might be obligated to pay brokers' commissions and other fees from this larger sum. In the end, you might net the same amount or less than the firm's offer.

Any one of the leading relocation companies is providing a service to your employer for a fee, and its primary goal is to satisfy you; this, in turn, cements the relationship with its client, your company. The relocation firm is not in the real estate speculating business of trying to buy your property for a song and to sell it for profit. Quite to the contrary. Do not feel intimidated. The firm is serving its best purpose if it can sell your home as quickly as possible after acquisition with a reasonable amount of effort, while holding down costs and management problems. Distinctive luxury homes might require more marketing time to obtain Top Dollar than is permitted under the firm's contractual arrangement with your employer. You will have to weigh carefully the amount of immediate cash offered against the many other personal factors involved before accepting or rejecting the proposal.

If your company has a home-buying service, homes in all price ranges are usually included for acquisition. There are usually no direct costs to you as an employee for this additional service, whether you accept the offer for your old home from the buying service or sell it yourself. You are eligible to take advantage of any or all of the services which your employer has arranged for by engaging a full-service relocation firm.

National relocation companies have offices throughout the country. Most do not directly employ real estate brokers or realtors. However, they do select those they feel are the most professional and reliable real estate firms serving the areas of their client's interest in all fifty states. It is to these firms that a family will be referred at its new location for the purpose of finding another home.

Most of my professional colleagues throughout America confirm my experiences with relocation/home-buying services as honest, sensitive, thorough, efficient, and fair organizations. They provide immediate and prompt service with a minimum of red tape and delay. Among those offering full relocation and/or home-buying service with major companies throughout the country are:

| *Name* | *Home Office* |
|---|---|
| Employee Transfer Corporation | Chicago, Illinois |
| Equitable Relocation Services | New York, New York |

| | |
|---|---|
| Executrans | Deerfield, Illinois |
| Homequity, Inc. | Wilton, Connecticut |
| Merrill Lynch Relocation Management, Inc. | White Plains, New York |
| Relocation Realty Service Corporation | New York, New York |
| Transamerica Relocation Service | San Francisco, California |

In the maze of problems normally associated with a family move from one part of the country to another, home-buying services do much to ease the financial and emotional strain of selling one's home. And part of that Top Dollar price is peace of mind!

# 20

## *So They Want to Take Your Front Lawn?*

As levels of government and utilities expand, so does the possibility of your home being acquired for public use. Eminent domain is the right of the government, or many of its agencies, to acquire your home or property for the building of a new highway, an airport, utility lines, a nuclear plant, or the like. This right is exercised through the courts by a process known as condemnation. If the courts determine that the proposed property is necessary for public use, they also must fix the amount to be paid to the owner. The law provides various guidelines—broadly defined and often misinterpreted—to determine what is a just and fair amount for the homeowner to receive.

Although the chances of becoming involved in a condemnation proceeding are slight, you should be well informed of the procedures to be followed in the event some government or public utility representative comes knocking at your door with a bulldozer parked in the driveway. Once it has been determined that your home is in the way of progress, there is little you can do to stop the wheels from turning and taking your property. But there is much you can do to get Top Dollar!

The laws governing the acquisition vary widely, but most condemnation proceedings consider severance damages, relocation expenses, highest and best use, and market value in the overall computation of the total to be paid to the dislocated—and often disgruntled and unwilling—property owner. Briefly, these considerations include:

*Severance Damages:* In the event only a portion of the total property is taken, an amount is awarded that represents the damages, if any, to the remaining property or its decrease in value.

*Relocation Expenses:* The homeowner, under some circumstances, is entitled to reimbursement of the cost involved in finding and moving to another home.

*Highest and Best Use:* As of the date of notice of taking, value must be fixed on the basis of the highest and maximum potential—reasonably justified. This is usually for residential purposes if the property involved is a home.

*Market Value:* This is the highest price a buyer is ready, willing, and able to pay and the minimum price the seller is ready, willing, and able to accept under conditions other than a forced sale.

The usual procedure in determining the price offered to the homeowner is for the government agency, public utility, or official acquisition unit to employ court-recognized appraisers. They will employ standard professional methods of appraising property to formally price the home involved. Their ultimate goals are to determine market value and highest and best use and to affix any severance damages, if applicable. The determination of the appraisers forms the basis of the preliminary offer.

The property owner usually has a reasonable time to accept or reject this preliminary offer. The mechanical proceedings for transfer of title vary with state laws and the agencies involved with the acquisition. In some states, the property owner is divested of title simply by the acquiring agency's filing a formal notice, map, and deed description. Recognizing that the taking of property under eminent domain has been harsh and unfair, many states are reviewing laws and regulations pertaining to the procedures involved.

The process is generally cold and impersonal, and what is most frustrating for the homeowner is the inaccessibility of the authorities who make the final decision. Furthermore, the condemnation process leans heavily in favor of the government. This is true because many state laws require that agency or utility to pay only part or all of the amount they offer, file the necessary papers, and give notice of eviction to any homeowner who does not accept that offer.

The law further provides that, with few exceptions, the property owner's only recourse is in the courts. Final determination by the court could take several years. This is a very costly procedure requiring the services of specialized attorneys, court-recognized appraisers, real estate experts, architects, engineers, and other specialists. If the final court award is more than the initial offer, the property owner is usually paid a reasonable amount of interest on the difference between what was paid and the final award. (The amount is computed from the day of the taking to the final settlement date.)

Under most circumstances, though, a homeowner should avoid going to court in a condemnation matter. Assume a governmental agency made a final offer for your home in the amount of $75,000, but you would not sell for less than $100,000 under any conditions. Let us further assume that your consultation with expert appraisers and attorneys justified your minimum-price conclusion but was not acceptable to the taking agency. If you resorted to the courts for this difference of $25,000 ($100,000 asking price less $75,000 offer), and were successful in your court action, chances are good that a portion of that $25,000 would have evaporated in the court costs involved. It is for this reason that, unless the difference between your offer and what you consider Top Dollar is substantial, it is essential to keep the negotiating process going in an effort to narrow the difference between the offer and Top Dollar asking price. This does not mean there are no costs involved in the negotiating process, only that they are usually minimal compared to those of a court action.

In general, however, the appraisers representing the agency in the condemnation follow strict guidelines and base most of their conclusions on what they are reasonably sure the courts will uphold. Do not expect to be compensated under existing federal and state laws for any labors of love you might have spent years of effort producing. Your home will be appraised primarily on the basis of what comparable properties have sold for in the past few years, even though yours might be an irreplaceable pre-Revolutionary gem.

Now that I have brought you to the brink of a nervous breakdown, consider the following procedures if someday you are faced with the threat of the loss of your home by condemnation:

- Remain calm! Your home might be one of many sites under consideration for the proposed project. Try to obtain as much pertinent information as possible from the taking agency before offering any of your thoughts, conclusions, or specific details relating to your property.
- Under no circumstances should you become involved in any negotiations pertaining to value or asking price.
- Join forces with neighbors who have also been approached —in a preliminary effort to share the mutual problem and the possible costs involved.
- The agency representatives who contact you are well trained in dealing with furious homeowners and they expect the worst. Try reverse psychology—be kind, gentle, and hospitable; listen, but say little.
- If it appears that your home is definitely involved in the taking process of the proposed project, your first move is to go to

your attorney. *Do not sign any documents whatsoever at this point.*

If your attorney is well experienced in condemnation cases, he or she will represent you. If not, you will be referred to an attorney or firm specializing in these matters. Your counsel will probably suggest that an independent firm of qualified appraisers, or one recognized by the courts in condemnation matters, be retained to determine the Top Dollar value of your property. Their conclusions must conform with the very technical guidelines admissible in condemnation court actions, and they may not necessarily reflect your opinion of the property value or the judgment of seasoned real estate professionals in your area who are not experienced in dealing with these problems. Upon receipt of all the facts and preliminary conclusions of the retained appraisers, your attorney will be in a position to make both a practical and a legal judgment, once the offer from the governmental or public agency has been formally presented.

Your attorney will most likely make every effort to obtain a better offer through negotiations, providing the appraisers representing you feel confident that the amount offered is not sufficient and is below the guidelines of property value (as could be reasonably documented in a formal court case).

The chances of your receiving a windfall profit are slim. There are exceptions—but very few. Consider yourself fortunate if you receive somewhere near Top Dollar. Attorneys skilled in these matters usually do quite well for their clients, as they are able to reach the decision-making people. Those in authority wish to avoid court action in most cases, due to costs and negative public relations. High government officials are much more sensitive to the homeowner's plight today than they were many years ago, and they will bring pressure to bear on the government agency involved to stretch policy as far as possible in order to pacify irate homeowners. Be guided by the advice of counsel, who will weigh the pros and cons of court action against a good compromise.

# 21

## *Keeping the Wolf Away from the Door*

Each year, thousands of homeowners are faced with the trauma of losing their homes due to personal financial crises. Prolonged unemployment, illness, marital problems, poor money management, and national disasters are the prime culprits in cases of near or complete financial collapse. During a downward trend in the economic cycle, certain large businesses and industries are forced to lay off great numbers of employees. Unemployment insurance and other benefits are barely sufficient to meet the basic needs, and it is during this crucial period that unemployed homeowners become delinquent in meeting their regular mortgage payments.

There is a stigma associated with a formal and public foreclosure action that normally reduces the value and marketability of a home. The process of a mortgage foreclosure is costly, messy, and usually the last thing a banking institution or individual holding the mortgage wants to face. Contrary to the opinions of many, bankers are not insensitive to the problems of delinquent mortgagors (borrowers), whatever the cause. In fact, most lending institutions will use every known method within the law before proceeding with a foreclosure action. They are well aware of the pitfalls involved in having to take ownership and possession of a home under forced sale conditions. In the event the value of the mortgaged property does not equal or exceed the amount of the mortgage balance due at the time of auction sale, the mortgagee (lender) becomes the owner faced with the problems of management and possession until such time as the property can be sold.

More than half of all foreclosures occurring each year might well have been avoided if the homeowner had taken certain steps prior to the world completely collapsing around him or her. Circumstances may become so severe that the only reasonable alternative is that the home be sold. In that case it should be sold, but not foreclosed. The difference between an orderly sale and a foreclosure might mean thousands of dollars above the mortgage balance due. This is money that could be used to liquidate other obligations, thereby avoiding the loss of future credit, and it could form the basis of a new start in life with dignity.

If at present you are going through some bad times, or face the possibility of falling into a financial crisis sometime in the future, and you must sell your home—do so at Top Dollar. The following guidelines are suggested:

- Contact your lending institution or the individual holding your mortgage during the period your payments are current, if you can reasonably anticipate a problem in meeting future obligations.
- Review in full detail the primary and secondary causes of your financial bind and solicit advice and guidance from the person or persons familiar with your particular home and situation.
- Discuss your status with an attorney, accountant, or public agency offering money-management assistance.
- Involve your spouse and/or members of your household in the financial discussions with banks and others so as to seek

reasonable solutions to both immediate and future financial problems.

- Determine whether the mortgage-payment delinquency is of a temporary nature, with reasonable solutions, or if there is no light at the end of the tunnel.
- Be prepared to expose your entire financial status honestly to the responsible bank officers and to strive jointly to seek reachable goals.
- If it appears that your home must be sold, advise the lending institution that you will do so voluntarily, in an effort to achieve Top Dollar. Demonstrate your intentions by keeping the lending institution fully apprised of the actions taken. Request that they withhold any formal public notification of delinquency for a minimum of three months. During this time you should make every effort to make some payment, if at all possible.
- If you are able to anticipate a reasonable sale price, notify any or all creditors of your intention to sell your home. Ask for their cooperation by withholding legal action against you for the collection of obligations due to them. If your total debt, in addition to the mortgage balance, appears in excess of the funds that will be available after you pay your mortgage debt, have your attorney meet with all your creditiors to discuss a reasonable settlement or to work out a payment program once the house is sold.

The primary purpose of the above procedures is to avoid public notice of your predicament through the filing of judgments (liens) and foreclosures. You will need ample time to sell your home at the best price possible without the pressures and tensions of a forced sale.

You might want to consider refinancing your present mortgage or obtaining a personal loan from a commercial banking institution to provide sufficient interim funds and avoid any delinquency of obligations. This can best be done prior to loss of employment or another anticipated problem; it becomes most difficult at the height of a financial crisis, especially if your normal income has been reduced or cut off. Do not overlook the fact that your home today might be worth considerably more than your present mortgage obligation. Substantiate the present market value by retaining the advice of several local real estate professionals. This basic documentation is needed if you wish to refinance your present mortgage or obtain a personal loan.

You must avoid the point at which creditors become leery of your financial relationship with them and file judgments on public record against your home. If these amounts plus the mortgage balance due total more than what the Top Dollar price of your home would be, it will be impossible to transfer good title. The difference between the selling price and the mortgage due is known as your equity, and it is with this cushion that you will be able to liquidate in an orderly way and within a reasonable time after your home is sold, the balance due all creditors. That is why it is so vital to keep the lines of communication open with all creditors at all times during a period of financial problems. Ignoring bills and notices from those to whom you owe money only compounds your problems and leaves few options other than bankruptcy and financial collapse.

During the bad time period, do not neglect to keep your home in the best condition possible under the circumstances. The banking institution holding your mortgage will usually pay the necessary property taxes and insurance fees, so as to avoid major repercussions associated with nonpayment of these two very important property obligations.

Never before in the history of America has the number of people employed been higher. Forecasters of gloom and doom do not have a large audience among the millions living pretty well and receiving weekly paychecks. It is in this type of economic climate that the problems of the worst of times—illness, death, and other catastrophes—are lightly thought of by most and seldom provided for. The average homeowner with a mortgage is vulnerable to a personal financial problem or he or she could become the victim of mass unemployment associated with a major economic downtrend.

The basic law of human nature is self-preservation, and the home is the most meaningful symbol of that concept. The goal of a homeowner is to be at all times in a financial reserve position, so that if all normal income were to cease for a period of up to two years, sufficient funds would be available to meet any obligations that came due in connection with that home. Not only will such a cushion provide the bridge from bad times to recovery from a personal problem, it will also give the homeowner sufficient time to weather a national economic storm when home sales are lagging or not bringing Top Dollar.

There might come a time when you wish to sell for a multitude of reasons but must do so under less than ideal conditions and without the luxury of time on your side—due to financial pressures. Taking into account all phases of your present financial status, consider one or more of the following suggestions to protect "home base" should less than good times be around the corner for you or our country:

- Make an extra payment or two on your mortgage as frequently as possible, even though it might mean a bit of a life-style sacrifice for the time being. Set a goal of at least twenty-four extra payments (two years). Be sure to notify your lending institution of your intentions so that your record will be marked accordingly and the extra payments will be treated as prepayments and not solely as a reduction of principal.

- Set aside from savings, securities, or other liquid sources a sum equivalent to two years' mortgage and other miscellaneous payments in a special account earmarked specifically for this purpose.

- If savings or other sources are not readily available because of your present financial condition, consider borrowing from your commercial bank the amount for the two-year reserve fund. Use the proceeds to make the two-year prepayment on your mortgage. Be sure to continue to make your regular monthly mortgage and commercial bank payments on borrowed funds. This might present a readjustment of your present budget, but it is well worth the sacrifice.

- Investigate the possibility of refinancing your present mortgage, borrowing only the amount needed for the two-year reserve prepayment. Do so only if the cost is nominal and does not endanger your present interest rate, which is probably much lower than will be charged for the new additional funds. Do not be tempted to borrow more than you need under this program.

- Other sources for reserve funds might be life insurance policies with cash equity that do not require repayment of principal but only payment of interest; retirement or pension funds; and various collectibles—such as works of art—that might be used as collateral for borrowed funds.

The interest on borrowed funds is generally deductible for income tax purposes, providing you itemize your deductions. But be guided by your attorney or tax adviser in this regard. It is much easier to borrow funds, if needed, for the reserve prepayment while you are actively employed and economic conditions are satisfactory. Every effort should be made to repay as promptly as possible money borrowed for the creation of this fund. Another major advantage in prepaying the mortgage from the fund is that it clearly establishes a triple-A type of credit history that comes in mighty handy during the periods of economic reversal.

A mortgage that has been prepaid for a few years provides an attractive selling tool during periods of high interest rates and mortgage tightening policies. The seller of a home to a Top Dollar buyer is in a position to offer an attractive financing package by providing this equity as part of the down payment requirement. It might also provide the new owner the opportunity of a one year or more "no payment" on the mortgage.

Anticipate the rough times. And, in warning you to do so, I can't emphasize enough the need for you to develop and maintain a close relationship with your mortgage banker. Perhaps it's nothing more than a periodic note telling him how you are doing in business—or maybe a photo of your new rose garden. *Any communication* is definitely the key to warding off problems later on.

Unfortunately, far too many people think that, when they have any transaction with a bank, they're dealing with a cold, removed, impersonal institution. Not so. Why, I've served on the board of directors of a leading money-lending institution for more than twenty years, and I can tell you that bank officers are not all that different than you or I. They know what inflation is all about; they've got the same problems themselves. And, believe me, they're the first to be compassionate when you come to them with such a problem.

However, remember, you must tell them what is happening if you're having trouble meeting your mortgage payments. You can't just stick your head in the sand out of embarrassment—or get an unlisted phone number. As I say, these folks will be the first to try to help you, even if it means refinancing your mortgage until you can get through this tough time. Yet, if you must sell, they'll also be the first to help you get your Top Dollar for that home.

But let's hope that never happens. Provide well for the lean times, and the foundation of your home will not likely crumble.

# 22

## *Sometimes the Sale Does Not Go Through*

Without exception, every homeowner who has ever decided to sell has done so as a born optimist. In thirty years of experience, I have never once met a seller who was not absolutely certain that at least two dozen anxious buyers were just waiting to put ink to a contract. And this they believe even though there may not be a nickel's worth of mortgage money for miles, their chimney is crumbling, and their well has gone dry.

Furthermore, even the most savvy of real estate people often share this unwarranted optimism. (Why else would they be in the business if they didn't believe that there is someone, somewhere out there, for every home on the market?) As long as there are people, there will be dreamers. And, although in this situation it may result in a healthy case of the blind leading the blind, it needn't always be so.

Sometimes the seller may be only too aware of the particular "problems" surrounding the sale of his or her home. Other times it is the broker/realtor who may view the situation clearly but who, for fear of antagonizing the client—or potential client —may be hesitant to paint anything less than a rosy picture. Indeed, it seems that criticizing one's home comes painfully close to criticizing one's child.

And yet, some professionals will tell it as they see it, and it is the seller who either refuses to accept what they are told or, worse yet, knowing, refuses to do anything to avoid the "problem." As a result, these are the folk who soon find themselves the victims of returned binders and deposits, a voided contract, or a closing that does not take place, none of which needed to have happened.

Sure, I admit that selling a home, especially today, is not a simple matter. It does take a great deal of organization, attention to detail, professional guidance, patience, perspective, and, in many cases, the blessing of the Almighty to make it work. For instance, take a minute to look at 101 of the many reasons, all taken from actual case histories, why your sale may not go through.

1. Application for the buyer's mortgage was rejected by the bank.
2. Termite condition of the home is in an advanced state.
3. Main source of drinking water is polluted.
4. Sewage system was not approved by the Health Department.
5. Wiring system doesn't meet the state code.
6. "Working fireplaces" are found to be not working.
7. Two acres, when surveyed, turned out to be only one.
8. Architect for the buyer didn't give his approval.
9. Real estate taxes were $1,800, not $800, as represented.
10. Liens and judgments against the property were more than the sale price at the day of closing, thus no closing.
11. Part of the seller's garage was found to be on his neighbor's property.

12. Seller was found to be mentally incompetent prior to closing.

13. House burned to the ground.

14. Buyer and his wife separate; one of them disappears.

15. Ditto the seller.

16. Title company finds a major discrepancy that must be cleared up *before* the property can go on the market.

17. Parents of the buyer change their mind about offering a down payment.

18. Buyer's wife becomes pregnant; house is now too small.

19. Seller's wife has a nervous breakdown and refuses to move at the time of closing.

20. Seller incorrectly assumed the broker was to be paid by the buyer.

21. "Small pond" was found to be an overflowing septic tank.

22. Passing motorist passes through the living room bay window on the day of the closing.

23. Prior to closing, a three-day torrential downpour takes care of the nice dry cellar—along with the buyer.

24. Zoning law changes the week before closing; no longer can the prospective buyer run a part-time beauty parlor.

25. Announcement of an atomic power plant site in the immediate area causes the closing to explode.

26. Buyer did not realize that an "abandoned" railroad track behind the home wasn't.

27. Seller finds it impossible to obtain a mortgage release from the individual holding it; he's on an extended safari throughout deepest Africa.

28. Rural telephone company can not furnish a private line for the would-be purchaser, a CIA agent.

29.  Buyer discovers that three antique light fixtures that "went with the house" have been replaced with flashlights.

30.  Seller did not think that the wall-to-wall carpeting was included in the sale; buyer did.

31.  Buyer discovered that the water line for the town runs underneath the home of his dreams.

32.  State decides to take the "south 40" in order to widen the interstate highway.

33.  Construction begins for a fast-food restaurant on a "nice empty lot" across the street.

34.  Buyer does not appear on the day of closing—he has not been heard from since.

35.  Buyer's down-payment check bounces.

36.  Buyer's down-payment check was stopped. Reason: none.

37.  Tornado-like winds blow the house onto the neighbors' property.

38.  Buyer did not like the seller's attorney. Seller did not like the buyer's attorney. The attorneys did not like each other.

39.  Mother of the bride urges an annulment if the bridegroom insists on buying the property.

40.  Seller overlooked the fact that he had given six months first refusal to someone else.

41.  Buyer could not obtain insurance coverage equal to the selling price.

42.  Banking institution appraised the seller's home at $15,000 *less* than the buyer had agreed to pay.

43.  Buyer was kidnapped and is being held for ransom.

44.  Septic tank was found to be less than 100 feet from the well, thus the application for mortgage fails to meet the approval of the FHA or Veterans' Administration.

45.  Seller's attorney took three weeks to prepare the contract;

buyer considered that two weeks too long.

46. Seller assumed that his brother who had a half interest in the property would be delighted to sell; he wasn't.

47. Minor earthquake cracks the foundation walls of the home only days after signing the contract.

48. Chaos results when a delivery man pours fuel oil down the drinking well by mistake.

49. Buyer files a petition of bankruptcy just prior to the closing.

50. Seller agrees to paint the home before closing; buyer not pleased with the shade of pink used.

51. Buyer has a heart attack; seller has a stroke.

52. Professional appraisers retained by the buyer submit a report literally filled with less than desirable findings.

53. Buyer finds that soil taken from the backyard, once tested, is not suitable for his hobby garden.

54. Buyer's child throws a rock through the neighbor's picture window while his parents are inspecting the property... and that took care of that.

55. Seller's German shepherd removes part of the buyer's leg: good law suit, but no sale.

56. Buyer discovers that school taxes for the property have increased by $700 since he signed the contract.

57. Local newspaper announces that "County Buys Sanitary Landfill Site" only 1,000 feet from the property line. Four years later, the house is still on the market.

58. Gasoline becomes scarce, and the buyer decides not to move to the suburbs.

59. Home mortgage interest rates go through the roof and hundreds of contracts become null and void.

60. Buyer fails to obtain township approval to pasture a herd

of milking goats on the front yard of the seller's home.

61. Buyer fails to have sufficient funds to cover unexpected costs at the time of closing.

62. Buyer refuses to pay the seller for 400 gallons of fuel oil on hand at the time of closing.

63. Seller simply refuses to close on the sale for any one of another 100 reasons.

64. Buyer's decorator objects when the "original wide-board floors" are uncovered and found to be nothing more than plywood.

65. The heating boiler blows up on the morning of the closing.

66. Close inspection discloses that the "five-gallon-per-minute drilled well" is actually a spring with a noisy pump.

67. Highbrow buyer balks when he discovers that the area is not served by cable television.

68. Bats in the belfry...everthing flies but the contract.

69. Buyer's wife spots a large black snake crawling out from under the old stone home; he crawls out of the contract.

70. Buyer's mother-in-law is mugged in front of the home on the evening she was to give her final approval.

71. Local power company announces that mammoth poles carrying dozens of power lines are to be erected nearby; buyer is shocked.

72. Power in the home goes off, the furnace stops, and all the pipes freeze up...and so does the buyer's writing hand.

73. Buyer and seller shake hands during the week. Buyer returns with his family on the weekend, hears the noise from the nearby stock-car racetrack and refuses to listen to anything more.

74. Seller fails to calculate the capital gain tax on the sale of his home and withdraws from the agreed contract price.

75. Contract voided when the seller's new home is still only

three-quarters completed by the day of closing.

76. Sale of the buyer's home does not go through, thus he withdraws.

77. Severe snowstorm delays the seller's moving date for more than a month. Buyer freezes and cancels the deal.

78. Buyer unable to enroll his children in a nearby private school as anticipated—no sale.

79. Local zoning board refuses to give the buyer permission to read palms out of the front parlor room.

80. Friends of the buyer find him the "perfect home," only he fails to see it as such.

81. Buyer B offers the seller $2,000 more money on the morning he is to sign a contract with Buyer A. Buyer A refuses to match the offer and withdraws. Then Buyer B has a change of heart and also withdraws. In this case, the bird in the hand—and the bird in the bush—flew away.

82. Seller actually believed that his present mortgage balance —what he still owed the bank—was the buyer's obligation, *in addition to the sale price.*

83. Buyer was led to believe that the in-ground swimming pool was heated. It was, but only by solar energy on days of 90-degree temperature or more.

84. Seller removed the "portable" toolshed prior to closing— that swift action removed the buyer.

85. Seller's neighbor arrived unexpectedly at the closing, informing all that half of the stream presumed on the property being sold belonged to her. Bank refused to issue a mortgage, and the seller and his neighbor later charged each other with assault.

86. Electric power lines serving the property had been privately installed years ago and never turned over to the public utility. Buyer refused to assume permanent maintenance unless

the power company agreed to service the line: estimated cost, $12,000. Buyer lost all power to proceed with the contract.

87. Buyer discovered that the seller had given easement for an underground telephone cable many years back, and he never called again.

88. Buyer discovered that the seller paid others for the rights to his water supply; the deal sank.

89. When construction began on a 200-foot communication tower located on a mountain top overlooking the home under contract, the buyer ceased all communication.

90. Buyer demanded the return of his deposit when informed that "the lovely home next door" was, in actuality, a rehabilitation center for paroled rapists.

91. Buyer agreed to purchase a home that consumed 4,000 gallons of fuel oil annually when the price per gallon was only 46 cents. Before the closing could take place, two things happened: the energy crisis and the contract crisis.

92. No one bothered to tell the buyer that the dead-end road leading to the property was neither town-owned nor town-maintained. Annual cost of maintenance and snow removal: $2,000, too much for this man.

93. Seller subdivided his home and ten acres from his entire property and found a willing buyer all *before* applying to the local authorities for permission. Naturally, permission was denied, and the sale did not go through.

94. Seller agreed to correct an inadequate water supply by drilling a new well prior to closing. Four dry holes—and $4,000 later—his buyer also went down the drain.

95. Upon invitation of the seller, the buyer takes a dip in the home's heated swimming pool and, due to faulty wiring, is

nearly electrocuted. Contract, too, goes into a state of shock.

96. Seller permits the buyer to move into the house *before* the closing date. As a result, nearly everything that could possibly go wrong did, including the sale.

97. Seller decides to withhold one acre after having agreed to sell the entire parcel at a specific price, and at the same time, he's also unwilling to accept a lower figure for the reduced acreage. Consequently, he still has the entire property—and no buyer in sight.

98. Seller agreed to have the unsurveyed property surveyed— until he discovered how much it would cost.

99. Seller agreed to hold the mortgage and the buyer agreed to pay 12 percent interest. Seller's attorney announced that the state usury rate limited interest to 10 percent, and the disgruntled seller decided to wait for a buyer with cash.

100. You really didn't think there could be a hundred reasons why a sale may not go through?

101. Well, you certainly won't believe there could be a hundred and one!

And yet, as you know, there are many things that can make —or break—your home sale. Thus, it should be reiterated that it is *your* job to stay involved, to anticipate the worst, and, whenever possible, to help pave the way for a problem-free contract to closing.

Of course, much of this responsibility does lie with your duly appointed real estate professionals, attorneys, and accountants. However, if you expect to get top results, you are going to have to demand top performance of everyone involved. But be prepared to back up that demand with a thorough knowledge of the situation. Granted, no one likes a sidewalk superintendent, let alone an ignorant one, but, if leaning over someone's shoulder is what it takes for you to get your Top Dollar, then by all means lean!

On the other hand, keep in mind that it does take time to sell a house. In fact, even under the best of conditions, it may take six months, a year, or even longer to find your one true Top-Dollar buyer. So, if that person doesn't step across the threshold the day after the "For Sale" sign goes up, don't panic, and certainly don't drop your asking price. Doing so will not stimulate new interest. Deciding if your original price is too high can only be done after a substantial number of potential buyers have offered 15 to 20 percent below that price. Or, if there are few offers, perhaps you and your realtor should determine whether the price is the obstacle, or whether those who have seen your home simply did not like it, regardless of the price. Now, if you still feel your home is reasonably priced, then stick with it, allowing, of course, some flexibility.

If, however, you have methodically followed every single suggestion in this book and still there are no serious offers, then take my advice: Close the play for at least four months. Take your house off the market, audition an entire new cast of performing professionals, and open to a brand new audience. In many cases, this is all it takes for a Top Dollar hit.

Remember, too, that nearly every home ever listed is sold— eventually. So, when things do not seem to be going particularly well, remain calm, even cheerful, and, above all, cautiously optimistic.

Good luck!

# 23
## *A Special Invitation*

Believe me, the last page of this book is written with great reluctance. We've covered a lot of significant ground. That is the obligation of a book such as this. Yet, just as important, I have wanted to impress you with the seemingly minor, sometimes even intangible, aspects of selling a home; the things that most sellers pay little attention to but that, in the long run, make the difference as to whether Top Dollar is achieved or not. That has been my real intent.

Yes, I have truly enjoyed our visit, and I thank you for inviting me into your home. In parting I would only like to say, if you have any question about the material covered within this book, or if you wish to share a specific problem, please write me, c/o Times Books, Three Park Avenue, New York, New York 10016. I welcome your comments and inquiries without obligation.